T J Higgs discovered her psychic powers as a child but, owing to discouragement and a difficult upbringing, it was not until many years later that she really took flight with her gift. Today, she is one of the most successful mediums in the UK. She has appeared on TV in shows such as *Psychic Private Eyes* and *The Three Mediums*, and her work is featured widely in the media. She is the author of *Living with the Gift* and runs her own centre for psychic development in Essex, UK. See www.tracyhiggs.co.uk for more information.

D1439721

SIGNS
FROM THE
AFTERLIFE

How the Other Side Can Comfort and Inspire You

T J Higgs

LONDON • SYDNEY • AUCKLAND • JOHANNESBURG

3 5 7 9 10 8 6 4 2

Published in 2010 by Rider, an imprint of Ebury Publishing
A Random House Group Company

The Random House Group Limited Reg. No. 954009

Addresses for companies within the Random House Group can be found at www.rbooks.co.uk

A CIP catalogue record for this book is available from the British Library

The Random House Group Limited supports The Forest Stewardship Council (FSC), the leading international forest certification organisation. All our titles that are printed on Greenpeace-approved FSC-certified paper carry the FSC logo. Our paper procurement policy can be found at www.rbooks.co.uk/environment

Mixed Sources
Product group from well-managed forests and other controlled sources
www.fsc.org   Cert no. TT-COC-2139
© 1996 Forest Stewardship Council

Printed and bound in Great Britain by
CPI Cox & Wyman, Reading, RG1 8EX

ISBN 9781846041983

To buy books by your favourite authors and register for offers visit www.rbooks.co.uk

The stories in this book are based upon real events. However, some names and details have been changed to protect the privacy of those involved.

While every effort has been made to contact all copyright holders, if any have been inadvertently overlooked, the author and publisher will be pleased to make the necessary arrangement at the first opportunity.

For my Nan, Elsie Irene Higgs, and my Grandad, Stanley Richard Higgs, and to my friend Didier Boyer – thank you for blessing my life with your signs.

Do not stand at my grave and weep,
I am not there, I do not sleep.
I am in a thousand winds that blow,
I am the softly falling snow.
I am the gentle showers of rain,
I am the fields of ripening grain.
I am in the morning hush,
I am in the graceful rush
Of beautiful birds in circling flight,
I am the starshine of the night.
I am in the flowers that bloom,
I am in a quiet room.
I am in the birds that sing,
I am in each lovely thing.
Do not stand at my grave and cry,
I am not there. I do not die.

MARY ELIZABETH FRYE

Contents

Acknowledgements

This book wouldn't exist were it not for the help and support I received from a wonderful group of people.

Firstly thanks to the team at Rider and in particular Judith Kendra and Sue Lascelles for their support and professional guidance. I'd also like to thank my literary guide David (aka Garry Jenkins) who once again made writing this book a fabulous experience. And I would like to offer a heartfelt thanks to all those clients and friends who contributed their stories. Each of them has enriched this book and for that I really am very grateful.

I would also like to thank my friends and family for their continued love and support. I would like to give a special mention to my nephews Thomas, Owen 'little O' and my gorgeous niece, Demi, who brighten up my life. My thanks to Richard . . . for always seeing my light. And of course I'd like to thank the two stunning men in my life – my two boys James and Ryan, of whom I'm immensely proud.

TJ xxx

Prologue: Seven Signs

In the spring of 2009, I went through one of the most emotional periods in my life when my beloved nan, Elsie, passed over.

The loss of a grandparent is always hard to bear, but saying goodbye to Nan, my father's mother, was especially hard for me.

We had always been very close. In many ways she had been my mother when I was a young girl. My own mother had, for various reasons, been a distant figure and I had spent a large part of my childhood in my grandparents' house, around the corner from our home in north London. I'd dropped into Nan's most days on my way home from school. It was in my nan's kitchen that I spent some of the happiest times of my childhood.

It had been in my nan's house that I had my first psychic experiences as a young girl, although at the time I'd not known what they were. There I'd seen the spirit of Pops, Elsie's dad, my great-granddad James, after he'd died. I'd also sensed other presences, although I'd learned to keep quiet about them. While my mother discouraged my interest in the spirit world, my nan had given me her quiet support. I think she simply wanted me to be happy and to follow the right path in life, wherever it led me.

She had lived to a ripe old age; she was ninety-one when she passed. Yet her loss was a hammer blow to me. I felt a huge gap in my life, like a fundamental part of me had been physically removed.

In the days leading up to her funeral I knew it was going to be difficult for me and my dad to hold it all together. But I was determined to do my best to support my dad and the rest of my family. Fortunately, my nan was there to help me . . .

Understandably I had been thinking about my nan constantly since she'd passed. You never know how some-one's passing is going to impact on you, or what thoughts are going to go through your head when you lose someone close. In my nan's case I found myself feeling desperate to know that she was safely with her dad, to whom she had been very close when she was a little girl. I don't know why I felt that way; all I know is that it became very important to me. In the days following her death and in the run-up to her funeral, I had this deep-rooted need to know that they were reunited.

I'd received a couple of intimations of her presence when I'd gone to see her in the chapel of rest a couple of days before the funeral. She'd been lying in her coffin in a rather characterless, windowless room. There had been a single candle burning alongside her.

I'd gone in and started chatting to her. As I did so, I noticed the candle begin to flicker strangely. When I was talking the flame was quite still and consistent. But then when I stopped and stayed silent it began to flicker like crazy. The candle was nowhere near me so it couldn't have had anything to do with my breathing and – as I say – the room was completely windowless so it couldn't have been a breeze or gust of air. I took it as a small sign from my nan that she was around.

I also noticed something else going on in the room. For obvious reasons, the temperature in any chapel of rest is kept very low, sometimes almost freezing cold. When I first stepped into the room containing my nan it had been as chilly as I'd expected. But within moments of my sitting down and talking to her, I began to feel myself warming up. Within a few minutes I was absolutely boiling hot, as if I was in a sauna. It was weird. Again, I took it as some indication of my nan's presence, with good cause at it turned out. In the months that followed I learned that whenever I felt her presence, which I did often, I would feel extremely hot.

As the day of the funeral arrived, I asked my nan for another, more tangible sign that she was there with us. Some mediums might hesitate to do this. The emotions of the day can be too intense and disrupting for spirit communication. But I put out my request for a very good reason. I'd been shown signs of the afterlife at funerals before.

A few years earlier I had lost another relative, Aunt Maisie, a relative on my dad's side of the family. My nan hadn't been up to travelling to that funeral, which was being held in the seaside town of Clacton. So she had asked me to go on her behalf.

I had been in my mid-thirties at the time but, curiously I suppose, this was the first funeral I had ever attended.

It had been halfway through the service that I had seen Aunt Maisie sitting on her coffin. She was quite a sight. She was wearing a white dress and was swinging her legs from side to side as if she didn't have a care in the world. She looked radiant.

I hadn't seen Maisie in years. Apparently, during her final months, when she'd been riddled with cancer and clinging to life, she'd been reduced to a pale shadow of her former self. That wasn't the woman I was looking at. She was sitting there with her hair looking gorgeous, a vibrant young woman smiling at everyone, except only I could see her.

Thinking back on it, I didn't have any bad emotions – in fact it was quite the opposite. I had to try really hard not to smile in front of the other mourners. It was odd and rather frustrating in some ways. Her sons and daughters, my cousins, were all crying while I was sitting there thinking, 'Well, she looks all right to me.' I wished I could have told them, but knew I couldn't.

Seeing Aunt Maisie like that was an important moment for me in a couple of respects. First and foremost, it confirmed my view that life continues, that our spirits go on to exist in another dimension. On a more practical level, it also helped me in my career. I was early in my training as a medium at that point, so it really encouraged me to press on with my development. It gave me renewed faith in what I was doing and made me even more determined to use my gift to help and comfort as many people as possible.

I knew there was a strong chance I wouldn't receive a similar sign from my nan because of the rawness of my grief.

One of the reasons I'd been able to see Aunt Maisie so clearly, I think, was that I'd felt slightly detached from her. Don't get me wrong, I'd loved Auntie Maisie and she'd looked after me sometimes when I was young. But she wasn't as close to me as my nan. My nan meant so much to me, I was in pieces about losing her. However, I knew that my loss could very easily act as a blockage to the spirit world, which is attracted to positive energy, so when I headed to the funeral I told myself not to get my hopes up. I couldn't expect to see signs from every person whose funeral I attended.

Nan's funeral was held at Lavender Hill cemetery in Enfield, one of the loveliest spots in north London – a huge, sprawling, tree-lined expanse of greenery. It was a bright, sunny and otherwise beautiful day.

The service was held in quite a small, old church. As we entered, I saw that the casket was standing next to a wall by the windows. Light was streaming through the stained glass, reflecting colours onto the wall. The curious thing was there were only two colours, not the usual rainbow mix. All I could see was green and pink. These were significant colours because they represent the heart to me.

I had put certain things inside the coffin. I don't want to divulge here what they are, because I want someone to give me that as a message one day. But they were also in green and pink. To me this was a promising sign. I began to feel the presence of the spirit world.

Pleased as I was to see this, however, I decided it wasn't enough and asked for my nan to show me more. She duly obliged. As I looked at the colours on the wall I saw them beginning to shift and take shape. As they did so I began to see my nan's face forming on the wall.

My reaction was immediate and obvious. I was holding my cousin Jackie's hands and I must have begun squeezing them really tightly because she suddenly looked at me. She saw my eyes fixed on a spot on the empty wall and she just said to me: 'You can see her, can't you? She's here.'

'Yes, she's here,' I said softly. 'She's here.'

My nan was very elderly when she died. The face I was looking at was still old, but it was also completely at peace. There was this real feeling of serenity. It was just a flash – she was there for literally a few seconds and then she was gone. But it was enough.

That was it – I immediately burst into floods of tears. It was a weird mix of grief and emotion and validation. But the tears soon subsided and I found the strength I needed to get through the funeral service and the warm, moving words that were spoken about my nan by the priest and family members.

As the service drew to a close we all began filing out of

the church and into the warm spring afternoon. My father and I decided to go for a walk through the large cemetery towards the plot where my nan was to be buried. Her father, my Pops, was buried there too.

For many years now I had been able to connect easily to the spirit of my Pops. He often came to me when I asked for help or guidance. His presence was a familiar one to me and suddenly I felt it again.

Enfield cemetery is very green and very well looked after. There are a lot of trees there, along with big ornamental statues and manicured grass. I was walking with my dad. He was really upset and our arms were linked together. We stopped to wait for my brother. We were standing in front of a metal water butt where people can fill up their vases.

Immediately I noticed that it had a number eleven on it. I knew immediately that was significant. I am a great believer in the powers of numbers and the study of numerology. The number eleven is a very spiritual number. It is, for instance, the number associated with Jesus. It is also the sign of a medium and I resonate personally at number eleven.

My nan had also lived at house number eleven on her street. So, as well as a floral wreath that said 'Nan', I had also bought a wreath in the shape of a number eleven.

Before I knew it, I felt the familiar itch on my nose. So I put out the thought: 'Pops, are you here?'

Well, at that precise moment, a little fat robin landed on the water butt. I will explain the significance of robins in more detail later in this book, but suffice to say I have for a long time associated them with my Pops. I was now certain this was a sign – or more accurately, a series of signs.

'Is Nan with you?' I asked.

At that precise moment another, slimmer robin landed alongside him. I couldn't have asked for a clearer sign.

What was one of the saddest days of my life had turned into one of the most amazing. In the space of a couple of days I had been given no less than seven signs from the afterlife, two in the chapel of rest, two more in the church during the service, and now three more out here in the grounds of the cemetery.

In truth, I desperately needed them. At the time I was doing very well in my career. I was about to begin *The Three Mediums* show at the Hammersmith Apollo. I had appeared on television and even had a book deal. But I felt like giving it all up because I was so overwhelmed by the loss of my nan. I had also lost a very good friend that same week. My friend, Didier Boyer, an amazing numerologist, had committed suicide days earlier.

My head was full of all sorts of questions. Why would someone so spiritual commit suicide? On top of the grief I felt at losing my nan, it was becoming almost over-whelming.

When I had been holding my cousin Jackie's hands, I had said to my nan: 'If you want me to carry on being a medium, you have to show yourself to me today. I don't think I will have the strength to carry on if you don't give me some kind of sign.'

She had given me what I asked for not once, but seven times.

As I will explain in this book, signs can manifest themselves in many ways. In the space of a single, emotion-filled hour, my nan had manifested many of them.

You, too, can experience them. You, too, can establish regular and meaningful contact with friends and loved ones who have crossed over to the Other Side. You, too, can see the signs. Provided you know where – and when – to look . . .

1 | Signs: an Introduction

What is a Sign?

I suppose the obvious questions to begin with are these: what is a sign? What does it symbolise? What is its meaning?

In its simplest form, a sign is a message. It is a sight, a smell, a sound or even a feeling that tells you a loved one is there, that their existence has continued on the Other Side. But it can also be a piece of guidance, advising you on what to do – or sometimes what not to do – at a particular time in your life.

The great thing about signs is that they offer a direct line to the spirit dimension. They cut out the middle man – or woman, in my case. This is because, unlike a detailed message in which a spirit communicates through a medium, a sign is something that is delivered personally to its intended recipient. You don't have to be in a theatre with a medium or a psychic. You don't have to be at a séance or in a Spiritualist Church meeting. You can be anywhere when you receive it: on a beach, a mountain-top, out shopping or simply sitting quietly at home.

For this reason, signs are the easiest and most universal method of connecting to the afterlife. In a sense, signs give everyone the opportunity to be a medium. They are there for all of us to receive.

Types of Signs

I am constantly amazed how many people come to me and tell me that they know *exactly* how their loved ones are going to make themselves known to them from the Other Side.

Often this will be based on something they said when they were still alive. 'When I come back to see you I will be a dog, or a bee or a flower.' So those they have left behind spend their time looking at dogs and bees and flowers.

A lot of people actually believe they are going to be physically reunited with the person who has passed over. They are convinced that the spirit of their loved one is going to physically materialise in front of them and say: 'Hello darling, I miss you.'

Don't get me wrong. I wish that were the case. It does happen in incredibly rare circumstances, usually in séances held by highly experienced mediums. For most people this is an unrealistic expectation, however. Coming through to us here in the physical world takes a huge amount of effort and energy on the part of a spirit. Materialising in that way simply takes up too much of that energy.

So the first important thing you must realise is that the spirit you are looking for is probably going to show itself to you in a much subtler, much more unpredictable way than you expect.

That's the bad news. The good news is that the spirit will use something that carries its own distinctive and personal signature. This may well relate to the spirit's personality while he or she was here in the physical world. So, for instance, someone who was passionate about football might display signs that relate to their favourite team.

There are lots of good reasons why this is the case, not least the fact that it is easier and requires less energy. In a way, it's an energy conservation thing. Think of it as the spirit of a loved one sending an email or a text rather than telephoning or coming physically to see you.

So, the sign might be the flicking off and on of a light switch or the television, the feeling that someone is stroking your hair or touching the top of your head. It might be a smell or a sound, a colour or a bird settling on a bush in your garden. In truth, it can be anything. In this technological age, it could be a text message, a twitter or an entry on Facebook.

The really good news is that once the spirit provides you with a sign and once you have recognised and acknowledged that sign, the lines of communication have been opened for ever. It is like learning a language. Once you understand it and master it, you can converse in it whenever you want.

Surprisingly, mediums haven't paid much attention to signs traditionally. Yet I think they are as powerful – and often more profound – than mediumistic messages through which the two dimensions, the spirit world and the physical world, communicate with each other.

Since I first became a medium I have encountered signs that have delivered a range of different information. As I say, on the simplest level they offer a simple reassurance that a loved one has safely crossed over to the Other Side. But they can also convey important information. They can guide you towards taking an important step or show you the right direction to take. They can tell you what *not* to do in a situation.

We are surrounded by the afterlife at all times. And each of us is being shown signs on a regular basis. This book is designed to help you to interpret and understand the signs that you are shown in your life. But it is also a collection of some of the most remarkable and significant signs I have encountered during my career. Some have appeared to me, many have appeared to other people. Each has conveyed an important message: that death is not the end; it is just the beginning of a new existence.

Sign Language: How to Ask for Signs

The spirit world is around us all the time. We can ask it for help and guidance at any time by asking for a sign and we will get an answer. But we must use this link to the afterlife carefully. It is not something to be wasted on trivial matters, or used like a free advice line.

You would not, for instance, put out a request for a sign to help you decide which coat to buy in the January sales. And you would not ask for a sign to show you what to have for dinner that night. Think carefully before you ask.

2 | Objects

The Four Pennies

There are many different opinions about the origins of the phrase 'pennies from heaven'. Some think it is a variation on the biblical phrase 'manna from heaven', meaning good fortune. Others believe that its origins are more modern, from the song of the same name which emerged from America during the Great Depression in the 1930s.

I really don't know who is right. But what I do know is that it refers to a phenomenon that is very common. In my experience, the appearance of coins – whether they are pennies, nickels, dimes or whatever – is one of the most frequent signs from the afterlife.

If you find a coin in an unusual or unexpected location it is a sign that the spirit world is close at hand or trying to get a message to you. If, for instance, you were to find a penny in an odd location, and it had the year of your birth on it, it could very well be a sign for you.

I have heard many amazing stories regarding coins, but one of the most remarkable concerned the Whittaker family.

One of the children in the family, a lady called Rebecca,

visited me for a series of readings shortly after her mother, Wendy, had passed over with cancer. Wendy's death had devastated her family but it had hit Rebecca particularly hard. She and her mum were very close.

It was clear from the beginning that Rebecca's family were very tightly knit. After I'd read for Rebecca, her dad, Reg, and her brother, Justin, came to see me. After that her sister-in-law, Emma, came to see me as well.

Almost always when reading for the family, I sensed Wendy's presence coming through to me within moments of starting. From the energy she was channelling through me I could tell she was a very vibrant lady. She'd only been in her early sixties when she'd passed over. There was real energy and personality in her messages to her children. I could tell that she was determined to reassure them about the fact that she had safely crossed over to the spirit world. They all received messages that their mum was at peace.

It was when Rebecca came to see me again, I think for the third time, that I gave what must have been one of the most memorable readings I'd ever done.

Her mother was showing me Rebecca's new partner, a guy she had been seeing for a while. I had sensed that Rebecca was keen to get some kind of message from her mother about this relationship. She wanted to know she approved and that she felt it was going to work out. As I connected to Wendy I was getting a very positive feeling. But then she began to show me something quite unusual. Suddenly my head was filled with images of pennies.

'Your mum is telling me that she has given you a sign about your relationship,' I said.

'What was it?' Rebecca said, suddenly looking quite excited.

'It's four pennies. They represent four months. And your mother is telling me that in four months' time that will tell you where your relationship needs to be. Either negatively or positively.'

Rebecca went white in front of me.

She told me that one night that week, before she had come to see me, she had been in bed with her boyfriend and when she had rolled over there had been four pennies on her back.

How on earth could that have happened if it hadn't been a sign? In what circumstances could there have been four penny pieces in someone's bed?

This wasn't the end of the message, however. There was something else Wendy wanted to tell Rebecca. Once more I started seeing pennies in my mind. 'There is definitely something happening with coins,' I said, smiling by now. 'Because she says she has also been throwing pennies at your father. I can see your father, Reg, sitting in a pub and he is having all these penny coins thrown at him.'

Rebecca looked a bit sceptical about all this but promised to check it out. It wasn't long before I heard back from her. She told me that she'd spoken to her father who had turned as white as she had when she'd learned about the coins in her bed.

'He'd kept having coins landing on him,' she said.

The first time it happened he was sitting in a pub, celebrating an anniversary of some kind, surrounded by family, and he just suddenly felt something drop at his feet. It was as if it had been thrown fiercely at him as if to get his attention. 'He'd looked around the pub to see who it was but there was no clue. He'd thought it might have been the effect of the drink and thought nothing more of it,' Rebecca said. 'But then a few days later he felt the same thing. The thing was that the coins all had dates on them that were relevant to him and my mother.' The dates were related to births and illnesses and anniversaries within the family.

It carried on for a while, happening not just in the pub but in other places too. But the difference was that from then on the family knew the coins were being sent from the spirit world. They collect them all now.

Recently the family marked five years since Wendy's passing. Her son, Justin, had by now begun developing as a medium and was taking part in classes at my centre. He was doing a class on the actual anniversary of her passing, when other members of the family were planning, as usual, to go to the cemetery. Justin is a lovely family man and when I met him at the centre he told me he was torn about being there. Part of him was thinking he wanted to be with his mum.

Fortunately, it wasn't long before he was shown that he was doing the right thing and shouldn't worry.

Firstly, on the day before his class a message had come through during another mediumship class. It had been

Wendy and she had said that her family were to know that there was no longer any need for them all to go to the grave each and every anniversary. They were to start getting on with their lives.

She also had a specific message for Justin. 'You don't need to go to my grave to find me. I am always here in the room with you,' she said via one of the other mediums studying at the centre. When he was told this, Justin visibly relaxed. You could almost see the weight lifting off his shoulders.

This was not quite the last part of his mother's communication with him, however. At the end of his class, as he was leaving through the front door of the centre, a coin just landed at his feet, as if out of nowhere.

It was a penny and he picked it up. It was marked 2005, the year his mother had died. When he picked it up and looked at it, his face broke into a broad, beatific smile. He knew exactly what it meant. It seemed Wendy was going to continue raining down her pennies from heaven for a while longer yet . . .

The Money Box

I've read a lot of stories from around the world about signs. Many of them have echoed experiences that I, or people I know, have been through. Examples of pennies – or other coins – being found in unexpected places are many, but a few stick in my mind.

One concerned a girl who had passed over at the age of only ten. She was killed when a car ploughed into her as she was coming home from school. Her parents were absolutely devastated. Life without her was extremely hard to bear.

But then they began getting signs that her spirit was still with them. In particular, they started finding pennies in the most unusual places.

The first time it happened, her mother was spring-cleaning the house and decided to wax the dining-room floor. She had moved all the furniture out of the room so that she had a clear space. She had then begun the process of waxing, beginning by washing the floor in preparation for the wax to be applied.

She finished washing the floor and left the room while it dried. No one else was in the house, so she was surprised when she returned to the dining room and saw something sitting right in the middle of the gleaming floor. She saw that it was a shiny penny. It couldn't have dropped out of her pocket because she didn't carry cash anywhere other than in her purse. And there was no one else in the house who could have placed it there. She simply marked it down as an odd mystery and forgot about it.

But then a couple of days later she had found another penny. Again, she'd been cleaning the house and this time had been scrubbing the sink in the bathroom. She'd left the room and then returned to see a penny sitting right in the middle of the sink.

By now she was sure something odd was going on. In the days that followed, she found pennies in the bath, on pillows and even on a freshly-made bed that she'd turned her back on for only a matter of seconds. Soon the family had become so used to finding pennies that they had bought a piggy bank and marked it 'Pennies From Heaven'. Every now and again she would have to empty it, so full did it become at times.

Even when they moved home, the pennies continued to appear. And each time they did, it reminded them of their beloved daughter.

A Friend In Need

Another wonderful story concerned a lady called Anne who began finding pennies in the most bizarre places.

The first one appeared one day as she went for a smoke. She'd pulled out a single cigarette and an extremely shiny and new-looking penny had fallen out with it. She'd shrugged her shoulders and ignored it, but soon afterwards she found one underneath her toaster at home. Weirdly, it had been attached to the base of the toaster with a small magnet.

By now she was getting suspicious. A few days later she had turned into bed after a long day. That evening she'd changed all the bed linen and was looking forward to slipping in between lovely fresh sheets. But instead she slid in and felt uncomfortable objects dotted around the bed. She pulled back the blankets to see four pennies lying there.

By now she was convinced there was something going on so she spoke to a spiritualist preacher. He told her this was a common form of communication from the spirit world. 'An angel is trying to contact you,' he told Anne.

It was a few weeks later that she discovered the likely source of the pennies.

Her best friend had recently lost her daughter in a traffic accident. Anne had been helping her deal with the loss as best she could, providing practical help and a shoulder to cry on when necessary. One day her friend had asked her to accompany her to the girl's grave where she wanted to clean up the plot and add flowers.

The two friends had walked up to the grave and begun cleaning when Anne saw something sitting on top of the headstone. It was yet another penny.

That night she found ten more at home. After that there was no question in her mind. It was the spirit of her friend's daughter passing on a sign that she had made it safely to the spirit world.

For a long time she'd felt unable to truly help her friend deal with her awful loss. She'd never been able to find the right words or do the right thing, or at least that's the way she felt. When she told her about the coins, however, it was as if she'd personally lifted the weight of the world off her friend's shoulders. She cried tears of joy at the news.

After that the pennies became less and less frequent. The message had got through. The sign had been read. The spirits had once more done their job.

The Wedding Bouquet

A few years ago, when I was starting my career as a psychic medium, I did a reading for a very attractive, bubbly, blonde lady called Clare. She came to see me at a difficult time in her life. She was only in her mid-twenties but she had lost her mother, Pat, eight months earlier and was missing her badly.

Clare's loss was painful enough, but it had come at a terrible time for her. Pat had died only months before Clare was due to get married. Clare and Pat had been very close and both had put a lot of effort into planning the big day. But Pat had been taken ill very suddenly and had passed over before she could see the fruits of their collaboration. Or, at least, that is what Clare assumed.

Pat's spirit was a strong and very forceful one, and I connected with her quite quickly. She was a very big personality and a very loving one too. I could tell immediately how much she adored Clare and the rest of the family she had left behind.

One of the first things she showed me was that she also loved David, the man who was going to become Clare's new husband. 'Tell David that I think he is the perfect partner for my girl and I love him very much,' she said to me. 'And tell Clare that while her last-minute doubts are normal, they are misplaced. She is doing absolutely the right thing in marrying him.'

It was a very emotional reading and at one point Clare began crying.

'I just wish she could be there with us,' she said. 'It just won't be the same now that she isn't there.'

When she said this I felt Pat's spirit become even stronger. I felt this real determination building up. 'Don't worry, I will be there,' Pat told me. 'And there will be a sign that I am with you on the day.'

'What sign, what does she mean?' Clare asked me.

Pat then began showing me the scene on the wedding day. I even began to hear music, 'Everything I Do' by Bryan Adams, which was then the Number One record in the charts. But it was the next detail that really stuck in my mind.

'You will know I am with you because of the bouquet,' she told me. 'In the middle of the floral arrangement there will be an odd flower, one that shouldn't be there and that you didn't ask for. Don't be upset by this because I will have done it. The odd flower will be the sign that I am with you.'

It was a very tearful and moving reading, one of the most emotional I'd done at that relatively early stage of my career. Clare left with her eyes still red from crying, but she made me a promise to stay in touch.

She was true to her word and a few weeks later I got a letter from her. In it she described what had happened on her wedding day.

She admitted that in the frantic days after our reading she had put her mother's message to the back of her mind for a while. It had been reassuring to know Pat approved of what she was doing and she'd overcome her nerves to complete all the preparations. She'd also rid herself of her eleventh-hour nerves and doubts about David. She had decided that he really was the man for her and she would marry him.

When the big day arrived she had placed a photograph of her mother on her dressing table and she had spoken to her regularly.

Midway through the morning, the florist arrived with the wedding bouquet. Clare had ordered white lilies but in the middle of her bouquet was an oddly-coloured flower. It was dark cream in colour and was a different type of bloom entirely. It wasn't a lily at all.

One of her bridesmaids spotted this and queried it with the florist. 'What's that doing there?' she'd asked.

But Clare had quickly intervened. 'No, don't worry, that's perfect – it couldn't be better,' she said.

The florist was hugely relieved. 'I had actually bought three of those flowers to break up the arrangement,' he said. 'But two of them died overnight. I was really torn over whether to leave the single bloom in there or not. If you'd said you didn't like it I would happily have taken it out. But it just seemed to be right that I kept it.'

'No, you did the right thing,' Clare said, before bursting into tears.

'What's wrong?' her bridesmaid asked her.

'My mum has just made my day for me,' she said, to perplexed looks from the florist and her family. They may not have understood what had happened, but Clare had.

In her letter, Clare told me that when she got to the church and walked down the aisle she felt like her mother was with her every step of the way. And, safe in that knowledge, she went on to have the happiest day of her life.

A Late Arrival

I could immediately sense the impatience in the male spirit who was trying to connect with me during a demonstration at the Hackney Empire theatre in London. His energy was really restless: it was as if he had made an enormous effort to get through to me and knew he wouldn't be able to keep it up for long.

To my relief, two women identified him from the evidence almost instantly. It turned out they were his wife and daughter.

His wife was overjoyed to be receiving a message from him. He had only passed over in the last couple of months and it was clear she'd endured a hellish time. Even from the stage I could see the drawn expression on her face. I felt for her.

I soon felt even worse for her, however, because it was clear to me that her husband's real interest tonight was not in talking to her. He was desperate to connect with his daughter.

'I don't mean to be rude, but he is worried we will lose the connection and he really needs to speak to her,' I told the lady. 'He's saying he needs to talk because he's going to miss her big day.'

Fortunately the mother understood. She sat down and handed the microphone to her daughter, a very pretty young woman, no older than twenty-one.

The daughter was very emotional as her father explained that he had been proudly watching during the past weeks as she got ready to marry her long-time boyfriend. He described in very accurate detail how he had seen her getting engaged. He talked about how he had watched her and her mother shopping for her bride's dress. She was amazed when he revealed that he'd seen her looking dreamily at some jewellery made of Swarovski crystals.

'I'm sorry I didn't leave you enough to get everything you wanted,' he said. 'But the jewellery you've chosen is beautiful and you will look beautiful too.'

I sensed that he was already fading so I focussed hard on getting across what I felt was his main message.

He assured his daughter that he was going to be there on the big day. He said that he knew they were going to have photos of him on the top table and that he was going to be toasted. He approved of this and was very pleased about it, he told them.

Both of them were crying openly by now.

As it began to peter out, the father's message began to remind me of the one Clare had been sent by her mother in the run-up to her wedding. In particular, the father had started talking about a floral arrangement – which immediately conjured up in my mind images of the bouquet with the single odd flower in the centre that had meant so much to Clare when she'd walked down the aisle.

'I can see your dad showing me a bouquet of flowers, but there's something about them that's late,' I said. 'They are either a bunch of all pink roses with one red one in the middle or the other way round, all red roses with one pink in the middle.'

I sensed the flowers had something to do with his son, who wasn't there tonight. I wondered for a moment whether, in his father's absence, he would be giving his sister away in the church. Before I could share that with the mother and daughter, however, the connection began to weaken. Soon the man's presence had faded away completely.

A camera crew were filming the performance that night. All those who had received a message were invited to sit down with them for an interview afterwards. The mother and daughter were among those who agreed. I joined them and had a chat.

They were very grateful to have received the message. 'It really means a lot to me,' the daughter said. 'It broke my heart when he died and I realised he wouldn't be there to walk me down the aisle. But now I know he will be watching over me that day. It will give me the strength I needed to go through with it.'

The one part of the message they didn't understand was the final bit about the flowers. 'That doesn't sound like my wedding at all,' the daughter said.

I was intrigued by this and wanted to know more. 'It was a very strong image he gave me,' I said. 'If I'm wrong about it, I'm wrong and I'll be happy to admit it. But I'd like to know what it means.'

So I asked them to email me if they could shine any more light on the matter. As they left the theatre, I wished them well for their big day and wondered whether I'd ever hear from them again. I soon got my answer.

I got home after the show at around one in the morning. As I got ready for bed, I noticed I'd already had an email from the mother and daughter. In fact it had been sent within an hour of their leaving the theatre.

I read the email quickly, dying to know what they had to tell me. It seems they had got home and spoken to the son that the father had mentioned in the message. He hadn't been able to make it to see my performance because he was in hospital with his girlfriend.

He told his mother and sister that he'd been really annoyed when he'd arrived at the hospital that evening. That night marked some kind of anniversary for him and his girlfriend and he'd ordered a lovely bouquet to be delivered to her the previous day. But she'd told him that the flowers had only arrived that afternoon, twenty-four hours later than he'd asked.

Both mother and daughter's ears pricked up at this. 'What sort of bouquet was it?' his sister asked.

'Roses, all red. Except they didn't even get that right. There was a pink one in the middle,' the son said testily.

The two women turned pale at this.

'What's wrong with you two – you look like you've seen a ghost,' the son said.

The daughter said that she'd given him a look as if to say 'well, yes, in a way we have'.

I saw immediately what had happened. The father had come through not just to tell his daughter he was going to be present at her wedding. He'd also made contact to tell them that he'd sent his son a clear sign that he was around.

He had made an enormous effort to get all this information across. But it had been worth it. When his daughter got married a few weeks later, she and her mother, and her brother too, felt his presence around them throughout the day. It was as if they were a whole family again. I felt very privileged to have helped them achieve that.

A Single Rose

Roses are a powerful symbol of love and devotion so, I suppose, it's no great surprise that they appear in messages more often than most other flowers. Not long after I learned about the father's sign to his son about his bouquet of roses, I met a family who had received a very similar sign – again involving roses. And, again, it involved a mother and daughter, but this time they had come to see me privately at my psychic centre.

Very soon after we began, I felt the presence of an elderly man. He was the lady's father and the daughter's grandfather. His name was Ronnie. Ronnie seemed a very contented soul. He wanted his family to know this. The two women, in particular the granddaughter, seemed a little intense, however. It was as if they were afraid of something.

As Ronnie continued to communicate to me, I began to understand why. His wife had died before him and he had been reunited with her in the spirit world. He showed me that his granddaughter had moved into their old house, which he was more than happy about. She had begun making some changes to the property and to the garden in particular.

Ronnie showed me an image of a memorial they had constructed for him in the garden. He said he liked it very much. The garden was Ronnie and his wife's real passion. They had spent hours and hours tending to it, Ronnie doing the heavy work and his wife overseeing the flower beds. It was this that the daughter was worried about, I eventually saw. She was worried because she'd dug up some plants and moved them around. She was scared that she'd done something that would upset her granddad. In particular, she was terrified that she'd moved her nan's rosebush to the wrong place. She hadn't killed it. But it was looking utterly lifeless and had been incapable of flowering when the spring and summer came.

Almost immediately, Ronnie began showing me a beautiful single pink rose. It was dark pink in the middle and a lighter shade of pink on the outside. It really was beautiful. 'He is telling me that there is a beautiful rose in the garden now,' I said.

The daughter looked shocked at this and shook her head, almost disappointed with me. 'There are no flowers on that rosebush. It's winter and look at the weather out there,' she said, gesturing at the cold, grey skies outside.

'I see what you are saying but he is adamant,' I said. 'He's saying that, as a sign from him, he is going to show you this bloom.'

'I really don't think that's possible,' the daughter said politely. 'But thanks for the message anyway. It was great to know granddad is in a safe place.'

Almost jokingly I said: 'Well, when you get home and you see it, you must send me a picture.' It didn't look likely but I have learned to trust the spirit world and to believe in their ability to deliver signs in the most unlikely situations. If they say something is going to happen, it will happen. And sure enough it did.

Facebook is a great tool. Within a couple of days the daughter had sent me a photograph of a single rose on this otherwise dead-looking bush.

It was really important for her. When you move into a relative's home and you change things around you want to know you've done the right thing. You want to know that everyone is happy. The spirit world had let them know that her grandfather was.

The Mirror in the Hall

Spirits will use whatever tools they can lay their hands on to provide us with signs of their presence. Sometimes we need to bear this in mind when we send out requests for help. Signs can be delivered in an unfortunate – and rather expensive – manner.

Take, for instance, what happened to the large and very costly antique mirror that I had bought for the hall in my home.

It was 2.30 a.m. when I was woken up by the most almighty crash. I ran out into the hallway to find my son James looking down the staircase into the hallway and repeatedly saying: 'Sorry, sorry, sorry.'

I looked down and all I could see was the beautiful mirror I'd bought at an antique shop a few months earlier, lying face down on the floor with hundreds of tiny shards of glass scattered all around it. I was really upset. My first

thought was how sad I was that this mirror had broken. It was about five feet by six feet in size and had a distressed, wooden frame. I really loved it, not least because it perfectly filled a space in the hallway.

I was also puzzled. The mirror always leaned inward against the wall. If it had been disturbed by a sudden movement or someone knocking into it, it should have simply slid down on to the floor face up.

But, as I could see all too clearly, it hadn't done this. It was lying face down, which was frankly an impossible angle for it to end up at. There was no way it could have got there unless someone had gone down there and physically thrown it over so that it fell in that direction.

I was still recovering from the shock of it all, when I noticed another figure emerging rather sheepishly from James's bedroom. It was his friend Jasmine. Jasmine was a frequent visitor to our house and often stayed listening to music and watching TV with James until late in the night. I often didn't know she was in the house when I came home from performing demonstrations and so I'd gone to bed tonight, unaware that she was here.

She looked even guiltier about the mirror smashing than James. She padded downstairs with him and helped him to clean it up. I left them to it. I was too upset to talk about it now. As it turned out, I would probably have been even more irate if I'd found out what had really happened.

In the morning James and Jasmine explained to me what they had been doing the previous night. Jasmine had been really upset by the death of her grandmother a month or so earlier. They had been really close since she was a baby. She missed her dreadfully.

Jasmine also had an interest in the spiritual and psychic world. She told James that she wanted some hard evidence that her grandmother was still around in a spirit sense. James had told her precisely what I would have told her. 'Talk to her in your mind and ask her for a sign,' he said.

So, she had done precisely that.

What Jasmine hadn't told James at the time, however, was that something odd had happened in her own home a few nights earlier. A tiny little vanity mirror that she'd had since she was a little girl had shattered suddenly for no apparent reason. She only saw fit to tell him this after the giant mirror in our hallway had been smashed.

James, like me, had immediately worked out what had happened. Jasmine's nan was using mirrors as her method of delivering signs. She was breaking any mirror she could find that was in a position to be broken.

After Jasmine had put out her request to her nan in our house, the spirits had clearly checked to see which mirrors were unattached to the wall. Every other mirror we possessed was fixed to the wall. The biggest and most cherished one was not.

Jasmine and James were incredibly apologetic about it and offered to save up either to fix the glass in the frame or to buy me a replica of the mirror.

I told them not to worry about it. Instead, I said to them that the best way to make it up to me was to promise they would think a little more carefully about what they were doing before asking the spirit world for signs in the future.

Every time I walked down the hallway for the next week or so I was reminded of the incident. Not because I felt Jasmine's nan's energy, nor because I saw any more signs of her presence – but tiny shards of glass kept showing themselves in every nook and cranny of the hallway.

Luckily, I don't believe in seven years' bad luck.

The Freight Train

Signs are intensely personal. A colour, a number, a name, an animal or an object that is significant to one person, may be completely insignificant to somebody else. This also means that anything can be a sign. A sign's significance lies purely in the eye of the beholder.

Over the years I've heard of people who look to all sorts of things to offer them signs. Few have been as unusual as the thing that my son, James, relies on for important guidance in his life: freight trains.

When James was a little boy, my then husband was stationed with the army in Yorkshire, where he was originally from. We spent some time with his family there, including my husband's grandmother, Ivy, James's great-grandmother.

One of the things James enjoyed most as a little boy at that time was watching trains. There was nothing unusual in that, of course. Most little boys love trains.

Luckily for James, his great-grandmother Ivy's house backed on to a railway line. He would spend long, blissfully happy hours looking out of a window in a back bedroom watching the trains passing by. Given that the railway line served some of the factories and coalmines in the area at the time, most of the trains he saw were freight trains. For some reason, as he grew older and began to take an interest in the psychic world, he began to regard them as important. Time and again, he would see freight trains at significant moments in his life. So now he uses them as a means of calling on the spirit world for help.

Many years later, while we were living in a cottage I used to rent in the Essex countryside, he was having trouble making his mind up about a relationship that he was involved in. He couldn't decide whether to break up with this girl or to give their romance another chance. But, rather than read a self-help book or go on the internet for romantic advice, James turned to the spirit world.

He thought he knew what to do but he still wasn't sure, so one morning he simply put out the thought: *if that's the right decision, please show me a freight train.*

Now, the village we lived in was near a train line. But it was a very different part of the world to Yorkshire and there was relatively little freight train traffic passing up and down that track. In fact, I'd be hard pressed to remember ever seeing a freight train passing by, certainly during daylight hours.

James put out the thought as he ate his breakfast in his pyjamas. Having finished he went back upstairs to his bedroom to get dressed. His bedroom window was at the back of the house and gave him a good view of the railway line.

Once he was dressed, James drew back the curtains to let in the morning sunshine. At that precise moment he heard a rumbling sound in the near distance. He looked out and saw a massive freight train rattling through the village.

It couldn't have been any clearer. It was the sign he was looking for. His decision was made.

Sign Language: Feathers

Certain objects carry more significance than others. One of the most resonant is feathers.

Feathers signify that angels are among us. Now some people believe this is literally the case – that the appearance of a feather at their feet or in some unusual place means that there is an angel physically present.

This is not what I personally believe. I don't think it's as simple as that, but I'm not knocking the belief at all. A lot of people take great solace from their belief in angels, which can't be anything but a good thing.

My own personal view is that if you find a feather in an obscure place – let's say you climb into your car and there is a white feather sitting there on the dashboard or at your feet – then that is a subtler message from the spirit world. It means they are present, that they are available if you like.

Whichever way you look at it, it is a positive sign. That's certainly what I've felt when I have seen feathers fluttering down towards the stage when I have been demonstrating in a theatre somewhere.

It has happened quite a lot. In one or two instances, it could have been explained by birds nesting in the roof of an old building, but in the vast majority of cases this simply wasn't a possibility. The feathers had materialised from nowhere.

Whenever this happens I feel a real surge of confidence. It is incredibly reassuring. I know, feel and can see that the spirit world is there.

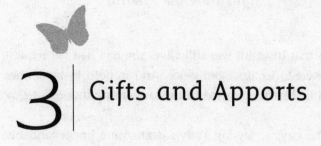

3 | Gifts and Apports

The spirit world is capable of manipulating our own dimension in many ways. A common phenomenon involves arranging gifts that bring enormous joy and relief to those who are missing or mourning loved ones.

The significance of the gift is rarely known to the person who presents it. And they are equally oblivious to the fact they have been expertly guided by spirit.

A Silver Star

A few years ago I met a lady named Brenda. She had lost her young son, Toby, a few months earlier.

Toby had been a very happy, healthy little boy until he contracted a rare lymphatic disorder. The doctors had been unable to do anything to arrest the spread of the disease. He had died within three months of its being diagnosed. His passing had shattered Brenda and the boy's father, as well as the rest of the family.

Naturally Brenda was in a very emotional state of mind when I met her. She admitted that she had been struggling to cope with her loss in the weeks following Toby's death.

But she had turned the corner when she had asked for a

sign that his spirit was still alive. She had had her request answered, not once but twice. And in both instances her sign had been delivered in the same form: that of a teddy bear.

The days following Toby's death were understandably tough. There were days when she didn't want to get out of bed, Brenda confided. But Brenda was helped through her grief by the love of her family and also through the support of a group of truly wonderful friends. She was overwhelmed by their kindness and warmth, she told me.

It had been one of her oldest friends who had delivered the first sign of the afterlife into which Toby had passed over. This particular friend now lived overseas and hadn't been able to get to the funeral. She hadn't seen Brenda for several years and had never met Toby. But she had been in the UK soon after the funeral and had decided to visit her old friend.

She had agonised over what card to give Brenda and, she told her later, had spent an hour in a card shop poring over hundreds of sympathy messages. In the end, however, she hadn't chosen a card at all. She had chosen a porcelain teddy bear. It was part of the popular 'Me To You' range and had a silver star on it. She told Brenda afterwards that she'd not been able to walk away from the teddy. Something had been telling her that she had to buy it.

When she gave the teddy to Brenda, she'd wondered whether she'd made one of the worst decisions of her life in choosing the bear. She was, at first, horrified by Brenda's reaction. Brenda had taken one look at it and burst into uncontrollable tears.

'Oh Brenda, I'm so sorry,' the friend said. 'I didn't mean to upset you.'

Brenda eventually composed herself and, when she had, she looked up with a big, beaming smile on her face. 'You haven't upset me,' she said. 'You have just given me the greatest gift I have ever received.'

What her friend didn't know was that when Toby was a baby the family had given him a special teddy bear. It was a 'Me To You' bear. Over the years, Brenda had bought one or two other bears from this range. Toby had loved them. But one of them in particular had been his favourite. It had a silver star on it.

On the night before Toby's funeral, Brenda had spent a few private moments alone with her son. It was her time to say goodbye for the last time. As she did so, she had slipped two items into his coffin. They were his most treasured possessions: a football shirt in the colours of his favourite football team, Tottenham Hotspur, and his beloved teddy bear with the silver star.

When Brenda told her friend this, it was her turn to shed tears. Again they were a mixture of heartache and joy. She felt the raw pain of Brenda's loss. But she also felt elated at having provided Brenda with such a powerful sign of her son's ongoing existence.

A few days later, Brenda was tidying up the house. She had, by now, put away all of Toby's clothes, belongings and toys. She would never forget him, of course, but she was ready to move on with her life.

It was clearly a decision that the spirit world – and

perhaps Toby himself – approved of. As she walked back into Toby's now empty bedroom, she looked around: she had hoovered the room the previous day and the cupboards were completely bare. But there lying in the middle of the carpet was a teddy bear. A 'Me To You' teddy bear.

APPORTS

One of the rarest and certainly the most dramatic signs you can receive is what is known as an 'apport'. This occurs when an object materialises in an unexpected place seemingly out of thin air. It has, in fact, been placed there by the spirit world.

I have heard of a number of dramatic cases of apports over the years. People have told me about objects, such as coins or toys or pieces of jewellery, suddenly appearing in the most unlikely locations.

Manna from Heaven

One of the most fascinating accounts of an apport I have heard concerned a famous medium called Helen Duncan.

Helen Duncan holds a unique position in the history of this country because she was the last person to be tried as a witch, under the ancient Witchcraft Act. Her story is controversial – and people are still arguing about it today.

She was an ordinary mother of six from Scotland, who had displayed her ability as a medium from a young age. What had really made her name, however, was her ability as a Spiritualist Materialisation Medium. This is a very, very rare gift which meant that, while in a trance state during a séance, Helen could produce ectoplasm containing spirits, which would then materialise and move around in her presence during a séance.

By the 1930s she was travelling the country, demonstrating her unique gifts to Spiritualist churches. Although she made very little money doing this, she always maintained that she only did it to support her children and her husband, who had been badly wounded in the First World War.

It was during the Second World War that Helen's gifts began to cause unease among politicians and the police. Understandably, during the war Helen's ability to connect to the Other Side became very much in demand. Families up and down the country wanted to know what was happening to their loved ones as they fought overseas. Helen was able to bring through uncannily accurate messages that not only proved their loved ones had passed over safely to the Other Side, but which relieved the stress and suffering of many grieving widows and families. In some cases, she was even able to summon up the physical presence of those who had died.

One man, Vincent Woodcock, who attended one of her demonstrations, described how he had seen, with his own eyes, his dead wife materialise in front of him and his sister-in-law. Not only that, but his wife had slipped off her wedding ring and placed it on her sister's finger, telling her that it was 'my wish that this takes place for the sake of my little girl'. Soon afterwards Woodcock and his sister-in-law were married and were later given a blessing by his first wife when they returned to visit Helen.

In 1944, Vincent Woodcock ended up giving evidence at the Old Bailey in what was one of the most contentious and strange court cases the old courtroom had ever seen.

There were those who disapproved deeply of what Helen did. As today, there were people who thought mediums were fraudsters, only out to line their own pockets. Helen had come to the attention of the police because of her popularity. As the war drew to a close they saw their chance to arrest her.

In one of her demonstrations Helen was contacted by a sailor who had recently passed over when his ship, which he identified quite specifically as HMS *Wareham*, was sunk. When news of this demonstration somehow reached the authorities they acted.

Officially, the War Office hadn't announced anything about the sinking of HMS *Wareham*. As far as the general public was concerned, the sinking hadn't happened. So, to have a medium talking about the ship and the loss of its entire crew was a breach of the Official Secrets Act. Helen was arrested and charged with spying.

At the time, the authorities were in the midst of planning the most secret and important operation of the entire war, the Normandy landings. Many believe that they had seen Helen's ability to see events; that they were terrified she would predict the landings and that somehow her reports would reach the Germans. Their suspicions were partially based on what was known about Hitler using mediums.

The spying charges were eventually dropped but Helen was tried at the Old Bailey instead under a centuries-old law banning witchcraft.

She was found guilty and was sent to Holloway prison where she spent the rest of the war. Of course, the prison walls couldn't stop Helen connecting with the spirit world and she continued to hold séances until her release.

There are several fascinating aspects to Helen's story, not least the part that Winston Churchill played. Churchill apparently harboured a fascination with spiritualism and attended séances. He was also ordained a Druid. There are those who believe Churchill actually visited Helen during the war. There is some evidence to suggest that he went to visit her in Holloway where, according to various sources, he promised to make amends to her when she was released.

What happened for certain was that, in 1951, when he returned to government as Home Secretary, Churchill's only major piece of legislation was to abolish the ancient 1735 Witchcraft Act which he believed had been used wrongly in Helen's trial. It was replaced by the Fraudulent Mediums Act, which paved the way for the recognition of the Spiritualist Church in 1954.

If Helen had thought that was the end of her troubles with authority, however, she was sadly mistaken. In November 1956 police decided to raid one of her séances in Nottingham. It was during that raid that she picked up the injuries that killed her.

It is one of the golden rules of spiritualism that a medium must never be touched when they are in a trance state. As I have seen myself during séances, when a medium enters this state they are extremely vulnerable indeed. If someone jolts you out of a trance state, you can cause terrible damage to your body. This is what happened to Helen.

Apparently police burst into the room where she was in a trance, pulled her out of her state, then strip-searched her in an attempt to find theatrical props. Despite the fact that she was clearly in deep distress they took endless flash photographs. They found nothing, but their action left Helen in extreme pain. A doctor was summoned and found she had suffered second-degree burns across her stomach. Some have speculated that this was caused by the ectoplasm that was coming out of her, forcing itself back inside her body when the raid occurred.

She was taken to a hospital in Scotland but died five weeks later at the age of fifty-nine in December 1956.

Today there is a growing campaign for Helen Duncan to be given an official pardon. In the age of the internet, more and more people are learning about the miscarriage of justice that she suffered. I think it's only a matter of time before her name is cleared. I am sure the spirit world will play their part in seeing that justice is brought to bear.

It was a séance that Helen conducted before her imprisonment in Holloway which presented one of the most amazing examples of an apport that I have encountered.

She held the séance in London and made contact with

a spirit who had passed over at a German prisoner of war camp. He spoke of how hungry everyone was at the camp, where their captors were keeping them on starvation diets. Some men were dying because of the lack of food.

I don't know exactly what Helen said during this particular séance but what happened later at the POW camp is recorded in the letters of one of the prisoners there. He described how, around the exact date of the London séance, food began mysteriously appearing in the British prisoners' quarters. It didn't just appear once, it materialised many times over the course of the following days. At first the prisoners were unsure what to do with it, suspecting some kind of German trap. But they soon began eating.

According to the POW in his account of his time in the camp, the German prison guards couldn't understand how the British prisoners suddenly started putting on weight and generally looking more and more healthy.

Even the spirit world was on the right side, it seems.

Sign Language: Don't Ask, Don't Get

The spirit world needs some encouragement too. Our guides, spirits and loved ones need to know that we are there too. It's up to us to do our part. It's all very well to say I'd like my nan to speak to me, but are you speaking to your nan? The most important aspect to using signs is understanding that you have to request the spirit world shows them to you. It really is a case of: don't ask, don't get.

4 | Birds and Animals

BIRDS

Birds have a particularly powerful association with the spirit world. I think this has a lot to do with the fact they fly so far above the ground, that they inhabit the air and the elements. In a way they straddle this physical world and the spirit world. They are somehow closer to it.

As I have said before, everything is subjective in what I do. The meaning of a particular bird to me may be subtly different from the meaning it has for someone else.

Because I work with Native American cards a lot, if I see a bird like a crow, for instance, I wouldn't be thinking about devastation, which is the association that many people make. For me it's about introspection. Because that's what a crow means in Native American medicine lore. To me, a crow signifies that it's a time for reflection and a time for thought.

So, if I were constantly to see a crow, I would think it's time I had a good look inside or took time to have a proper think about things.

Similarly with their relative, the raven. Because we

associate them so strongly with the Crown jewels and the Tower of London, ravens are – to me, at least – about protection. So if I kept seeing a huge raven, I would think I might need some spiritual protection around me.

There is a guide later in this chapter to one or two other birds that play a significant role in delivering signs from the spirit world.

A Bird In The Bush

A few years ago I was in the process of looking for a new home. It marked an important moment in my life. I had been through a difficult period personally, but was beginning to see a new way forward. I had begun to develop my gift as a medium and was looking forward to happier, more rewarding and fulfilling times. Finding the right place to live was one of the keys to achieving this. I needed to find a sanctuary, a place I truly felt at peace.

Much of my unhappiness had been to do with the fact that, along with my two young sons, I had been living in a council house on an estate where we really didn't fit in. All three of us had grown to loathe living on the estate and we had each suffered bad experiences there. So in many ways I was looking for something that was as far removed from that place as possible. I needed a home that would banish all those bad memories and allow us to start afresh.

As part of my development as a psychic and medium I had learned how to tap into and draw support from the spirit world. In particular, I was getting regular guidance from my great-grandfather, James, or Pops as I liked to call him. He would appear to me in various forms on a regular basis. Sometimes I would hear his voice, whereas at other times I would physically see him standing nearby. On other occasions, he would offer me signs of his presence. And I had felt his presence very strongly as I had looked for my new home.

One day, my estate agent called me up and asked me if I would like to visit a cottage in a small, pretty little village in the Essex countryside, not far from Stansted Airport. It sounded ideal, if a little outside my price range. Something about the way the agent described the cottage touched a chord within me, however. I felt that I didn't really have a choice in the matter: I simply had to go and see it.

The omens were good the moment I set foot inside the cottage. I immediately felt the presence of not only my Pops, but also my nan Elsie's husband, my granddad Stanley. His name, Stanley, often appears to me when I ask for a sign. Sure enough, as I began looking around the cottage with my friend Amy, there it was on the name of the cooker in the kitchen.

But it was in the garden that I got the most telling and meaningful sign. As I have mentioned, birds often have an important role to play in delivering signs from the afterlife, with specific birds signifying specific things. A lot of people associate robins with spirit messengers.

Pops was the first of my spirit messengers and had remained one of the most important. Maybe it wasn't surprising that, because of his importance to my relationship with the spirit world, I had often seen my Pops as a robin. Whenever I needed any reassurance that the spirit world was nearby, I would consciously look for one of these little birds. I would send out a thought, asking for a sign, and on many occasions I had been rewarded with the sight of the word 'robin', an image of a red-breasted bird or – occasionally – a sighting of an actual robin.

Now, in Essex, I really liked the inside of the cottage. It was just what I was looking for in terms of its size and atmosphere. It was a cosy, comfortable and – above all – peaceful place. As the summer was coming, I was also keen to have a place with a nice garden, so after inspecting the rooms inside the cottage, my friend Amy and I headed outside the back door.

The garden was a smallish but well-tended area. The first thing I noticed was a massive, purple bush. And the moment I saw it I noticed something else. There, sitting in the middle of it, was a very brightly coloured and very fat robin.

I couldn't believe it. I had only just put out a thought to my great-granddad. I'd said: 'If this is the right place I need to see a sign from you, Pops.' And here he was. Amy realised the significance of the robin immediately and took a photograph.

The plucky little bird continued to keep its eye on us the rest of the time we were in the cottage. By now I was fairly certain this was the home I had been looking for, so I gave the rooms another tour. Whichever window I looked out of, I would see the robin. It was as if it was following me. It was almost as if it had come along just to say: 'You are going to live here.'

At the time I had no idea how I was going to be able to afford this place. The rent was well beyond what I'd planned to pay. But after that incident, I knew that I had to live there. If, as it seemed, I was meant to be there, the spirit world would find a way to make sure I managed the monthly payments.

And so it proved. The cottage was to be one of the happiest homes I'd ever lived in. And it was while I was living there that my career really began to take off.

A Woodpecker on the Heath

A few years back I used to read for a rather elegant and sophisticated lady, called Elspeth, who lived in London.

She had first come to me a couple of months after her husband, Peter, had passed. They had been married for more than thirty years, tying the knot when they were both in their early twenties, so his passing had really knocked her for six. She felt lost without him, she told me once.

Peter came through in the very first reading. He told her he was safe and at peace in spirit, and that he was often watching over her. She was delighted by this. Elspeth admitted that she still talked to him every day. 'I didn't want to feel like I was wasting my time,' she told me.

I told her what I tell all my clients. The more you keep your loved ones in your heart and your mind, the more chance there is of them delivering you a sign or a message. 'Keep talking to him,' I said. 'And he'll keep talking to you.'

And so it proved.

Elspeth began coming to see me frequently. Peter always came through, sometimes more clearly than others. Almost always, however, he showed me a particular image. It was of Elspeth out walking a dog.

'I keep seeing you walking on a large expanse of green, it's not just a typical park. It's a big area,' I said to her once.

She nodded. 'That's Hampstead Heath, near where we live,' she said. It was a lovely little dog with a moustache on its face. It reminded me of Lady, the dog in the Disney film *Lady and the Tramp*.

Each time I saw them walking together, however, I also saw something else. It was a bird, a woodpecker. Wherever they went, it was there, almost tracking them.

As a medium, you build up a spirit vocabulary, and woodpeckers were a familiar part of mine. A woodpecker used to live near my cottage in Essex and early on I received a message in which it appeared in relation to someone's romantic life.

Then, one particular friend went through a difficult time with the man in her life. My local woodpecker appeared quite often while this was going on. Each time it did, I would ring my friend and tell her to expect a development in her relationship. Invariably, she'd be on the phone within twenty-four hours to tell me her man had rung, they'd met and talked, or that some kind of decision had been made. It was quite uncanny. When her relationship finally ended, the woodpecker seemed to vanish from my garden and I have seen it only fleetingly since.

However, from then on whenever I have seen – or heard – a woodpecker again I have regarded it as a sign that something significant is happening either in my own relationships or in those of my close friends.

Armed with this knowledge, I explained the connection to Elspeth now. I also told her that her husband said she was a lady who wouldn't necessarily notice an ordinary bird, like a sparrow or a robin. It would have to be an unusual or an interesting bird to get her attention.

'I think this woodpecker is a sign that your husband is listening to you as you talk to him. I think this wood-pecker is the spirit world's way of saying, "Keep talking to me,"' I said. This really brightened her up and she beamed as she heard this.

The next time I saw her, Elspeth told me that she had gone straight home from that reading, grabbed the lead from the kitchen and taken her dog out for a long walk around Hampstead Heath.

'There's a particular spot where I stop and sit, looking down over London below me. I often talk to Peter while I'm there,' Elspeth said. 'I did it that day and I told him what you'd told me,' she said.

She'd not seen it immediately, but on the way back up to the top of the heath she had looked up into a tree for some inexplicable reason. There, pecking away at the bark was a small woodpecker. It stopped and seemed to look at her.

She put out some thoughts, some questions she wanted to ask Peter. In the calm and quiet of the late afternoon, she felt something coming back. It was a magical moment.

She'd never really noticed a woodpecker during her walks on the heath before. From then on she would see one almost every day.

She knew that it wasn't Peter in an incarnate form. She understood that it was simply a sign of his presence in the spirit world. But it helped her turn the corner in her earthly life without her husband.

She didn't feel so lost any more.

Sign Language: A Guide to Other Bird Meanings

As you become familiar with the signs that are sent to you from the afterlife, you will gradually build up your own spirit vocabulary, as I have done over the years. In the meantime, I'd like to share with you some of the meanings that I have discovered.

Swan

Swans famously mate for life. So, for me, swans are all about love and relationships. If you seem to be seeing pictures of swans wherever you go, you might be receiving a sign about your love life. If you are looking for a sign in connection with an everyday relationship, for instance, and you keep coming across swans, then this could be a good validation of your relationship. It is a reassuring thing.

Seagull

For me, the appearance of seagulls is connected to our emotions. This is because the birds are attracted to water, which signifies the emotional side of life. They are also slightly scatty birds in that they are not very grounded. And they are always rather loud and noisy. So, for me, a seagull doesn't suggest calm emotions. If you are asking for signs and you see seagulls in unlikely or unexpected places, this could signify that your emotions are all over the place and need to be sorted out.

Magpie

The old wisdom says that, when we come across magpies, we're to count 'one for sorrow, two for joy, three for a girl and four for a boy'. So whenever we see a magpie we should always look for a pair. The magpie is connected with different superstitions in many cultures – for instance, in Korea magpies are said to be the bearers of good news – so it might not necessarily be an unlucky bird for you.

Eagle

These are the creatures that are perhaps closest to the spirit world, especially according to Native American lore. Because they can fly higher than almost any other bird they have a connection to the divine; yet they still return to the earth so they are grounded in this existence too. As a result the eagle represents balance and the power of the spirit world. So if you were to see an eagle in an unexpected place, it could be a powerful sign that the spirit world is close at hand.

Hawk

Hawks are the bird equivalent of Mercury, the messenger of the ancient Roman gods. To me, hawks symbolise the power of observation, of being able to see and understand what is going on around us. So, seeing a hawk could be a sign that you need to take a good, hard look at those around you.

Raven

Many cultures around the world associate the raven with magic. I believe that a raven can symbolise a change in consciousness. But it can also be a sign that prompts us to try to understand ourselves better. If you see a raven and feel frightened or intimidated, it may mean you need to learn about your innermost fears and demons.

Robin

Many people believe that robins have strong links with spirit messengers. Plucky and full of character, these birds are also associated with the qualities of joy, divine sacrifice (because of the robin's red breast) and spiritual rebirth. Gypsy lore connects them with good luck.

ANIMALS

Like birds, animals have an ability to deliver powerful signs from the spirit world. It is something that is recognised in shamanic cultures around the world. Societies like those of the Native American peoples believe in the concept of 'totem animals', in which a spirit is believed to take the form of an animal in order to communicate with us through dreams or visions. It is something I have experienced myself, particularly during my early development as a medium, when I repeatedly dreamt of panthers, a common spirit animal messenger. Later in this chapter, you will find a guide to the powers associated with some of the animals that can often appear in our dreams and visions.

It's also the case that some people seem to have very strong animal qualities about them, and can remind us of particular creatures.

Two Foxes

A man called Barry, who was my very first circle leader, has always reminded me of a fox. If I see a fox in unusual circumstances, I will immediately connect it with Barry and tread carefully. I know he is sending me a message or a warning of some kind.

The most amazing example of this happened when I was driving through a nearby town during a terrible spell of weather. Rain had been falling for several days, causing widespread flooding in the area. Ordinarily I wouldn't even have got in the car in that weather, but I'd had to go and see a friend who was in a terrible state, having lost her mother the previous week.

As it happened, the weather had eased off a little during the half-hour drive. But I could see that water had settled by the roadside and on the radio there were news bulletins about rivers bursting their banks and communities being cut off by the waters. I knew there was a river running through the town I was visiting, but had seen no evidence yet of it having risen so high that it had flooded the streets.

To get to my friend's house, I had to go through the middle of the town. The traffic was pretty light so I was able to drive quite quickly. But, as I headed towards the turning I needed to reach the estate where my friend lived, I suddenly felt a strong premonition of needing to slow down. It was almost as if someone was flagging me down in my head.

I'd barely been able to digest this when something else distracted me. All of a sudden two foxes appeared. They weren't together. They appeared from either side of the road. What one fox, let alone two of them, was doing out scavenging in the streets of a country town in the middle of rainy weather, I had no idea. But I knew they were there.

The two foxes then proceeded to walk out into the middle of the road. Once there they stopped; they looked at me before running away again. 'What was that all about?' I asked myself.

As I turned the corner, I suddenly found the street flooded. It looked like the water level was rising even now. I could see another two cars had come to grief there and had been abandoned. One of them had water up to the bottom of its windows. I could see a couple of distraught people pointing at one of them as it slowly disappeared under the water.

I had to react fast. Luckily I was able to stop the car and reverse out. If I'd gone in another few yards I'd have been two or three feet under water.

Once I'd got safely out of there, I said a little thank-you to the spirit world. If I'd carried on driving at the speed I had been, there is no question I'd have driven into deep water. The two foxes had saved me.

Two Kittens

I was sitting in the reception of the psychic centre that I run in Waltham Abbey late one morning when a frail-looking lady walked in through the door. She must have been in her late seventies.

It had been raining outside and for a moment or two she stood in the doorway struggling to shake the water out of her umbrella. As I watched her I immediately got a very strong sense of an independent spirit, a woman who lived on her own.

I looked at my appointment book and guessed she was my midday appointment. The only name down in the diary was Esther. 'I assume you must be Esther,' I said.

'That's right. And you must be Tracy. I've heard a lot about you,' she said.

She was twenty minutes early for her appointment. On another day this might have been a problem, but I'd had to be elsewhere during the morning and she was my first appointment of the day. I didn't have another one until early in the afternoon. So I ushered her upstairs to one of the reading rooms and sat her down. I could sense a slight nervousness in her so got started on the reading immediately.

As usual with a new client, I knew absolutely nothing about her or her life. All I knew was her first name and what I had picked up from her when I'd first seen her come in downstairs. I didn't know what she was looking to find out from the spirit world. To be honest, that was just the way I liked it.

It didn't take long for a spirit presence to make itself felt. I could tell it was male, but I was finding it hard to pin down his age or anything else significant about him. There was something out of the ordinary about the vibrations I was getting.

I was then given a name, Topsy. It seemed an unusual name but I figured it could be a nickname so I relayed it to the lady.

'Do you understand the name Topsy?' I asked her, ready to see her shaking her head.

Instead she replied with some words that, in all my years as a medium, I'd never heard before. 'Yes, I do,' she said, beaming. 'Topsy was my cat.'

I had heard about this happening to other mediums, but it was the first time it had happened to me. I was connecting with the spirit of an animal.

I must admit I was quite excited by this, so continued the reading with extra enthusiasm. I wanted to see where this would take me. I still found it a challenge to interpret the vibrations I was getting. They were definitely different from those I had been used to getting from humans. But eventually I was able to convey one important message to Esther.

'He says that he is so pleased that you have got the two kittens,' I said.

Again, this brought a big, wide smile to Esther's face. In many ways, it was a familiar situation. Over the years, I have conveyed many, many messages to people who had been concerned about starting a new relationship, having lost a husband or a wife. They come into the reading room feeling guilty about moving on with their lives, but leave having been told how delighted their loved one is to see that they had found renewed happiness here in the physical world. It's one of the most pleasing things about my job.

This was what was happening here. Her cat was passing on the same kind of message: 'Don't dwell on my passing any more; I'm fine – get on with your new life with your new companions!'

Esther became more and more relaxed after that. For the rest of the reading she just enjoyed herself. When it came to an end, I carried on chatting to Esther for a couple of minutes.

'I had a feeling he was still around, living as a spirit,' she told me.

'Why?' I wondered.

'Because I'd seen some signs that he was with me still,' she said.

I was even more intrigued now. It was still raining hard outside and I had ten minutes to spare before my next appointment. Suddenly I was grateful that we'd got off to an early start. Now I had time to listen a little longer to Esther.

It turned out that she had indeed been given signs from her cat. And what was fascinating was that these signs were similar to some of the normal signs that human spirits send us.

There was a particular chair in Esther's living room that always used to be Topsy's favourite. There was an old cushion that sat on the chair. On a couple of occasions, Esther had walked by the chair and noticed an indentation in the cushion, as if someone had been sitting on it.

Also, when Topsy was alive no one else would sit on that seat because it had been *his* place. And it was the same now. People would come into the room and deliberately avoid sitting in that chair.

But perhaps the strangest thing was the way that some kind of force was taking charge of the kittens within the house. Esther told me that the kittens were very scatty normally, as kittens should be. But she noticed that every now and again they would stop misbehaving and almost stand to attention, as if they were being told off by a parent. She also noticed that they seemed to know when mealtimes were. Again, this was something that they were too young to know. It made her wonder whether there was a parental presence in the house.

She'd also felt an occasional touch on her leg when she'd been sitting down in her chair. It was that unmistakeable, slightly static-electricity feel of a cat brushing against her. The first time it had happened she'd assumed it was one of her two kittens. But when she'd looked in the corner of the room, she'd seen the two of them lying there, happily rolling around in a playful ball together.

The next time it happened there was no doubt in her mind that it was Topsy. She'd felt a funny atmosphere in the room, as if the slightest of breezes was blowing under the chairs. The next moment she'd felt that same, light, brushing sensation that she'd experienced before.

I was honest with Esther and told her that it was the first time that I'd had a spirit communication from an animal. And I told her that her description of the signs that Topsy had given her confirmed something that I'd suspected for a while: cats send and also receive signs and messages too.

I have cats as well. I love their combination of warmth and independence. I find them to be perfect, undemanding companions. But, as with all pets, they can break your heart as well as warm it.

I told her about a cat of mine called Tiggsie. He was a lovely cat, with a really great personality. I'd had him for a few years now and was very attached to him. He seemed to mirror my moods. That had never been more the case than a few months after he'd been born.

His mother was a cat called Mushroom whom I'd had for five years or so. Mushroom was a bit of a wanderer, which was hardly unusual for a cat. But she did have a habit of playing a little too close to the road that ran outside my cottage.

One day the inevitable happened. I was out at the time

and only learned about it afterwards. My son, James, told me that she'd been run over by a car. We were both devastated, as was Tiggsie. At the time, he was just a few months old, still a little kitten.

I put his mother's ashes in a wooden, cat-shaped ornament that I kept in the living room. Tiggsie obviously didn't know anything about this, or so I imagined. My view changed one day when I walked into the room and saw that Tiggsie had somehow managed to climb up on to the cabinet on which the ornament was standing. He was lying there, curled around the vase, with his chin on its lid.

I don't know what I felt most: amazement or emotion. I couldn't believe my eyes. I'd heard talk of animals mourning their loved ones when they pass over. Elephants, most famously, apparently grieve over their lost relatives and herd members for a long time. But I'd never seen a living example of this.

For a while after that, I'd been fascinated by the subject. I'd researched into the history of cats and seen how important they had been in ancient cultures, where they were regarded by many as divine creatures. The Egyptians had a tradition where, when a cat died, every member of the family shaved their heads as a mark of respect. There was even a city built that was dedicated entirely to cats.

It wasn't until I met Esther, however, that I began to understand the true scope of the spiritual existence of animals. Her message from Topsy, and the story she told me about the signs she'd received, changed my view of the spirit world on a fundamental basis.

It confirmed one of the very best things about my job. Every day is different. And I never, ever know who is going to appear in my reading room. Or in my communications with the spirit world either . . .

Sign Language: A Guide to Animal Meanings

Animals play a really important role in the interpretation of the spirit world. And they have been a subject that has fascinated me ever since I first began working as a psychic, reading Native American picture cards. Based on ancient medicine man traditions passed down through the ages, these cards feature a whole range of animals, from lynxes and bears, to eagles and butterflies. Each has a very specific meaning, which we can use to help interpret appearances by these animals when they form part of a spirit sign. Here is a guide to a few of the most common and important animals and their possible meanings.

Dog

Dogs are not known as man's best friend by accident. As a member of the Native American's extended family, the dog was a lookout and a helper. He was also intensely faithful to his human friends. So today we associate the dog with loyalty.

Mouse

The mouse is a symbol of scrutiny. This stems from the fact that it uses its whiskers to examine and touch everything around it. This can be a good thing and a bad thing. It is good to pay attention to detail in our surroundings but less so to dwell on things to the extent that we can no longer see the wood for the trees. If the sign you receive comes in the form of a mouse, it may mean you need to consider which of these states applies to you: either you are over-thinking a situation or perhaps you need to examine it more closely.

Lion

As the mythical king of the beasts, the lion is often connected with royalty. This noble animal can also symbolise bravery and generosity, linking with the proud yet kind-hearted sun sign of Leo. It appears on the Strength card in the Rider Waite tarot. The sign of a lion might indicate the need to hold on and find inner reserves of strength – perhaps the strength of your conviction.

Bear

The bear hibernates through winter, which may be why its symbolism often relates to dream states, introspection and the powers of the unconscious mind. It can also be a symbol of protective motherhood and of great personal power. The sign of the bear can also suggest the need to have patience. Like the bear, which hibernates a lot and changes during this period, so you too must be patient and await the spring and the new beginnings it will bring.

Wolf

In Native American teachings, the wolf is a teacher of new ideas. Independent yet loyal to the pack, the wolf embodies both caution and cunning. Because the wolf is a spirit teacher, a sign involving a wolf could indicate some kind of psychic awakening.

Horse

The horse is a powerful symbol in many different cultures. It is frequently connected with the elements of fire and water, and with the sun and the moon. It can be linked with ideas of freedom and vibrancy, as well as with sacrifice and personal quests. A horse can be a sign of the need for both stamina and control.

Cat

There is the well-known saying 'curiosity killed the cat' – cats are connected with independent thinking, with psychic powers and mysteries. The cat was a sacred animal of the Ancient Egyptians.

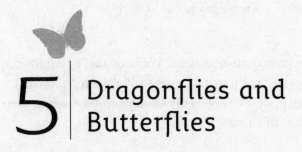

5 | Dragonflies and Butterflies

DRAGONFLIES

Animals play an important part in helping me, as a medium, to deliver signs from the spirit world. And different creatures play very different roles.

When I first began to understand and develop my gift as a medium, for instance, panthers were the most significant animals to me. I had begun to see them in my dreams. When I joined my first mediumship circle, it was explained to me that these animals were spirit messengers passing on very particular messages to me.

As I developed, however, panthers began to play a lesser role and they were increasingly replaced by dragonflies. The dragonfly carries great significance among Native American peoples. These beautiful insects represent illusion and what separates fact from falsehood. Their spiritual meaning is to reveal the truth. And that is what they have regularly done for me.

Dragonflies have played a hugely influential role in my recent life. They have delivered signs that, I'm convinced, have changed my life for ever. Without them I might not have appeared on television. Without them I might not have opened the psychic centre in Waltham Abbey that is now my pride and joy. Without dragonflies, I might even have died in a fire!

A Spirit Centre

The importance of dragonflies started to reveal itself when I was developing as a medium. I can see now why this was happening. The dragonfly symbolised what was happening in my life, the way I was stripping away the illusions I'd had about what that life was going to be and replacing them with the truth of what I was meant to do.

As this happened the power and wisdom that a dragonfly embodies began to make more and more sense to me. They are one of the oldest creatures on the planet. They are prehistoric creatures – they've always been here. Their generations of ancestors have seen more things on this planet than any of our ancestors have.

It was when I had established myself as a medium with my own centre in the town of Waltham Abbey that I saw how that wisdom was being directed towards revealing the truth of my future. In fact, if it hadn't been for dragonflies I wouldn't have found the centre in the first place.

At that point in my development, I already knew I wanted to give something back to the world of mediumship. So I decided to open a centre where people could teach and learn about every aspect of spirit communication. I'd set myself up in other people's premises in the past but now I wanted to find a base of my own. Finding a place hadn't been easy, however. But then, through a friend, I got to hear about a place that was available for rent in the centre of Waltham Abbey.

Looking back on it now, I can see that it was inevitable that I was drawn to Waltham Abbey. Waltham Abbey's history goes back to pagan times. I believe the abbey was first built on a pagan mound. Its spiritual links are many. There are, apparently, ley lines that run through the area.

When I first went to view them, I liked the office premises straightaway and was keen to take out a lease on them. But I also wanted to get a sign from spirit that it was the right place for me to be. The sign came in the shape of a dragonfly.

I was walking with a friend through the grounds of the abbey in the town one day when I felt something land on my shoulder. I looked down and saw that it was a beautiful, dark blue dragonfly. I didn't flinch – I wanted it to stay there, which they don't normally, but in this case it did. For a couple of minutes I walked around with it sitting on me.

That was that. My mind was made up.

It was at that point I knew not just that I was meant to be there, but I also knew what I was meant to call my centre. Which is why the sign above the premises now proudly says: The Dragonfly Centre.

As I settled in to work there I discovered that the town's links to dragonflies run deep. I began reading for a lady called Doris, who started to tell me about the history of the place. For instance, back in time, there used to be a giant metal dragonfly on the gates of the abbey. I also discovered that there are mosaic tiles around the abbey which include images of dragonflies. As if that wasn't enough, I then learned that there is also a dragonfly sanctuary nearby, too. Apparently thousands of them live on the marshland there. They are a protected species and scientists study them there.

I learned something else after I'd moved in as well. The meridian line, the invisible line that goes from Greenwich around the world, to mark the start and end of the world's time zones, runs right outside my front door. When I learned this I felt even more convinced I was in the right place. The Dragonfly Centre was a new beginning for me. It was a starting point. The fact that it stood at the spot where time starts was another huge sign. I knew I'd come to the right place. Everywhere else I had tried working hadn't really worked in the same way. There wasn't enough energy. Here there was. And it was soon drawing people in.

I knew I was there to stay.

The Turquoise Dragonfly

Perhaps the most dramatic moment I've had in association with dragonflies happened one day soon after I'd occupied the centre in Waltham. It took place when we were painting and decorating the rooms in the three-storey building. We had been at work in the upper-storey rooms and come downstairs to have a brief tea break.

By now we had finished the downstairs room which we had decorated with all sorts of psychic paraphernalia.

There were, for example, Native American dreamcatchers, made from feather and lightweight wood, hanging from the ceiling.

It was a lovely, summery day and we had all the windows open. Every day for a week or so now, this beautiful, turquoise-coloured dragonfly had flown into the shop. That in itself was a bit odd because they are not supposed to live for very long. This one seemed to be defying the rules.

Sure enough, it appeared again today and started fluttering around the room. We were just about to head back upstairs when it came to sit on my arm. For what must have been a couple of minutes, it just sat there with me. I started talking to it and for a crazy moment I thought it was talking back to me. It was a magical moment, having this creature sitting there. I felt like I never wanted it to leave.

Out of nowhere I heard a loud, sharp bang. All of a sudden the room was filled with the smell of burning and smoke. We rushed to the front of the building where we saw a light was on fire. Fortunately the fuse box was downstairs – in fact, it was right next to where I was sitting at the back of the building. We were quickly able to trip the main switch so that the power supply to the rest of the building was switched off. In the meantime, we put the fire out.

One of my friends gave me a look of shock. 'You do realise that if that dragonfly hadn't kept us sitting here next to the fuse box then we could have been in big trouble,' she said.

In the rush to sort the emergency out, I hadn't had time to think about it, but I immediately saw what she meant. The dragonfly had kept me and my friend sitting downstairs for a few minutes longer than we'd intended. If it hadn't arrived we would either have been at the front of the shop – underneath where the flash had happened – or, even worse, upstairs when the fire broke out.

Either way we could have had a much more serious situation. If we had been at the front of the shop we could have been burned by the exploding light. If we had gone upstairs or had been sitting elsewhere in the building we would not have heard the bang or smelled the burning. There is every chance the dreamcatchers and the other materials downstairs would have caught fire. Heaven only knows what might have happened in that eventuality. The centre could easily have burned to the ground.

Blue For Luck

In 2006 I received an interesting invitation. I was asked to go to an audition at the medium Tony Stockwell's studio in Wickford, Essex. A television company was looking for a female medium to present a new series that was being made.

I'd been working as a full-time medium for a while but I was unsure whether I wanted to make the leap into television. I knew I had a gift, but I wasn't sure if it was ready to be shared with the much wider world that TV would bring me.

On the day of the audition, I was really torn about whether to ring up and cancel. The audition wasn't due to be held until that evening, but I'd got up early in the morning fretting about it. By lunchtime I'd managed to work myself up into a right state. I could almost feel my temperature and my blood pressure rising. And then, out of nowhere, a dragonfly appeared.

It was a lovely deep blue colour and it hovered in front of me for a couple of minutes. It was as if the fluttering of its wings were acting as some kind of emotional fan. My emotions began to cool down and I became calmer. I also began to feel much more positive. It gave me the strength to go ahead and do the audition.

That evening proved to be one of the most significant of my life. It went so well, I was offered a role in the television series *Psychic Private Eyes* alongside two much more famous psychics – Colin Fry and Tony Stockwell. That paved the way for me to tour the country with Colin and then to go on and appear with Colin and Derek Acorah in the hugely successful *Three Mediums* shows at the Hammersmith Apollo.

If it hadn't been for the calming blue dragonfly, I doubt any of that would have happened.

A Sign before Midnight

Many of my friends associate me with the dragonfly. A friend in LA, Natalie, always sends me a message when she sees one. She says it reminds her of me.

Because of the dragonfly's links to illusion, it has also helped friends reveal the truth of what is going on in their lives. That was certainly the case when a close friend of mine, Shaun, needed some guidance a few years ago.

Shaun lived in New Zealand which is where I'd met him when I'd toured the country with my fellow medium, Colin Fry. Shaun had been our tour manager and had been very good at the job too. We'd stayed in touch.

Shaun was a very spiritual guy who placed great store by the omens and signs that he saw in his life. His only problem was that he never knew how to interpret them and invariably asked me to do it for him. I didn't mind, even though the time differences could be a bit of a challenge, given the fact he was on the other side of the world.

On this particular occasion, Shaun had rung me early in my morning to tell me that he had been getting lots of thoughts and messages regarding a new job that might be coming up. He desperately wanted to get into the mainstream entertainment business and in particular the movie industry. There were all sorts of hints and clues as to what might be in the wind for him. But he couldn't see his way forward, which was why he had called me.

'Tracy, I'm so confused. There is so much going on, how am I going to know what to do?' he asked me. 'I think I am going to land a really good job. But I need to know that now, so that I can be focussed on it. Can you ask for a sign that will show me that's right?'

I had a very strong sense that he was on the verge of something very good happening to him on the work front. I had seen some signs myself.

To Shaun, like my other close friends, I was represented by a dragonfly. So I told him that if this feeling was right then he would see a dragonfly before he went to bed that night.

While it was early spring here in England, it was high summer in New Zealand at the time, so there would have been a few dragonflies around. It wasn't impossible that he would see one. That wasn't enough for Shaun, however.

'A dragonfly,' he said, in a bit of a tizzy. 'Where will I see it? How will it appear to me?'

'Don't worry,' I assured him. 'If it's meant to be, it's meant to be. Just keep your eyes open and let me know.'

For the rest of my day I imagined him down there in New Zealand, walking around, looking for a dragonfly. Everywhere he went I was certain he was nervously waiting for it to appear and buzz him.

His night time was my afternoon. And as midnight approached in New Zealand I hadn't heard from him. We'd last spoken at 10 p.m. his time. 'I haven't seen anything yet, it's not going to happen,' he had said, in even more of a flap by now.

'Wait till midnight.'

Well, just before midnight his time I got another phone call from him in a very different mood. 'I've just seen it,' he said, yelling down the phone in excitement. 'I saw the dragonfly!'

It turned out that he had gone out for a late dinner with some friends who I knew as well – Mark, Angelica and Lisa. It was a lovely dinner party, apparently. Even though Shaun was slightly on edge throughout.

Right at the end of the evening, Lisa had brought some candles out and started to light them. Shaun was sitting on a sofa when he saw the candleholder in her hand. It was made of ceramic and had a large image of a dragonfly engraved on it.

Shaun had had to fight the very strong urge to grab Lisa and give her a kiss right there on the spot.

Shaun and I talked regularly over the next couple of weeks. As I'd sensed, events began to take shape that would change his life for ever.

One day, completely out of the blue, he got a phone call inviting him for an interview for a job in the movie industry. It wasn't really clear what the job entailed, but he went along anyway.

The interview went really well and he was offered the job. It turned out it was as an assistant to one of the world's biggest film directors, who was based in New Zealand at the time. Since then Shaun's career has gone from strength to strength.

Needless to say, he now regards the sight of a dragonfly as a good omen.

The Necklace

Two years ago I was approached to write a book. A couple of publishers had expressed an interest but I quickly formed a clear preference for one of them. I was invited to go and meet them, to see if we liked each other and whether I felt that we could form a working relationship. The morning I set off to their central London offices, I put out a request to the spirit world: 'Show me a sign that I am meant to be working with these people.'

After arriving at their swish offices near the Thames, I was ushered into a room filled with very smart-looking people. They all said nice things and made a convincing case for becoming my publishers. I was impressed but still hadn't seen the sign that I needed to push me over the edge and agree to sign with them.

And then I noticed a necklace that one of the ladies in the room was wearing. It was a dragonfly. That was that. Decision made.

I knew I was going to form a partnership with the people in this room. I had heard – and seen – enough to be sure.

The confidence I felt only grew in the weeks that followed. To mark the moment, a friend bought the exact same necklace for me. I was really touched by the gesture and loved the necklace. As I looked at it in detail I saw some things that I hadn't noticed before. As well as a dragonfly it had a snail and a flower incorporated into the design. The whole arrangement was set inside a circle. I smiled as I realised just how perfect this was.

The snail signified that things were going to happen slowly but surely. Just the way I wanted it. The flower meant it was something that was going to grow and grow, something that ties in with the meaning of the dragonfly too. The omens could not have been better.

BUTTERFLIES

Butterflies are among the most common animal signs of the afterlife. This is, perhaps, not so surprising. After all, they symbolise transformation, the journey from one stage of life into another. This is what happens, of course, when people pass over. They are transforming themselves from the physical beings who occupied this earthly realm, into the spirits that inhabit the eternal dimension.

The Orange Butterfly

I have heard of and witnessed many, many examples of butterflies acting as signs. But one of the most memorable involved two sisters, Hazel and Lily.

Hazel came through to me one evening during a demonstration in the Midlands. She was looking for her younger sister and quickly led me to a middle-aged lady called Lily, who was sitting towards the front of the auditorium. Lily was quite nervous at first but she soon relaxed. Hazel had some heartfelt things to say to her sister. She told her she was grateful for all she'd done towards her funeral, which she'd been pleased about. She also thanked her for remaining so strong for the rest of the family.

The main purpose of Hazel's communication, however, was to try to get a message through to her own daughter, Lily's niece, Naomi. From what Hazel had shown me, Naomi was only nineteen years old and had been completely shattered by the loss of her mother.

She'd been at university studying for her end-of-year

exams when Hazel had passed. The results were predict-
able. She'd gone to pieces and flunked everything,
although the university authorities had been generous and
allowed her to re-sit at the beginning of the next term.

Hazel was disappointed that Naomi wasn't present in
the audience tonight. Yet she gave me the distinct
impression that she knew where she was and she was soon
filling my mind with images that led me there.

Suddenly I could see a crystal-blue ocean and a giant
ship, carving its way through the waters, leaving a long,
white trail of waves in its wake. On board I could see a
young woman. I then saw a very, very specific image,
something that was so vivid and precise I could have
touched it. It was of a big butterfly, with brilliant, orange-
coloured wings, fluttering around in a blue sky and
skimming past the young woman's face.

She was dressed in a swimming costume and a wrap-
around skirt and was walking along the sun deck of the
ship. I could see the butterfly was following her. Every
now and again it would circle her head, brushing against
her long, brown hair and even, at one point, touching the
crown of her head. The girl was aware of the butterfly but
didn't seem troubled by it at all. In fact, it was making her
smile. I sensed that smiles were something of a rare
occurrence at that moment.

I described all this to Lily but it meant nothing to her.
She simply sat there shaking her head. 'Sorry, Tracy,' she
said. 'I don't recognise anything that you are talking about
there.'

As always, if I pass on information that doesn't make sense at the time, I asked her to check it out with other members of the family and to let me know if it began to ring true.

It was about ten days later that I got an email from Lily. I sat up in my chair the moment I started reading it.

Lily hadn't known it at the time of the demonstration, but Naomi had been on a Caribbean cruise a few days earlier. She had come round to Lily's house soon after getting back and told Lily all about it. Lily described how well her niece looked and how relieved she'd felt at the transformation in her. She looked tanned, relaxed and more at peace with the world than at any time since her mum's passing. Lily told her that she'd done absolutely the right thing in going off to the Caribbean.

The trip was more significant than Lily had realised. Naomi explained that, unbeknown to the rest of the family, she and her mum had planned to go on the cruise together. Hazel had booked it and paid for it soon after being diagnosed with her illness. But she'd deteriorated far more quickly than expected. She'd died just a matter of weeks before she was due to go on what she'd told Naomi was going to be the trip of her lifetime.

Lily told Naomi about the message she'd received at my demonstration. Naomi smiled at the thought of her mum coming through. But when Lily told Naomi about the butterfly she had looked shell-shocked.

'What day did you say you went to the demonstration?' she asked.

'It was last Wednesday,' Lily said.

Lily could see Naomi doing the calculations in her head. 'Wednesday? We were sailing that day and I spent all afternoon on the sun deck. That's where I would've been at the time you were at the theatre.'

Lily looked as shocked as Naomi.

When Lily asked her straight out whether she remembered seeing an orange butterfly, Naomi looked at her ashen-faced and nodded. 'Yes, it followed me up and down the deck for five minutes. I couldn't get rid of it. Not that I'd wanted to, there was something so beautiful about it,' she eventually explained.

For a moment the two of them had sat there shaking their heads. It had been Naomi who had broken the silence. 'How could she know about that?' she said, referring to the message I'd brought through. 'That's impossible.'

Of course, it wasn't impossible. It was quite the opposite of that. It was entirely possible, provided, that is, you believe in the spirit world and their capacity for connecting and sending signs to us.

There was absolutely no doubt in my mind that, far away in the Caribbean, the spirit world had sent Naomi a very powerful sign. In many ways it was the perfect symbol of how life can carry on beyond the grave.

Naomi had intended to go on that cruise to be close to her mother. And in the end, she had been. She had been as close to her spirit as she could have possibly wished . . .

A White Butterfly

As a demonstration at a theatre in the northwest of England drew to a close I felt the presence of a middle-aged lady growing stronger and stronger in my mind. I was aware of something else as well. It was an image of butterflies. Lots and lots of butterflies.

As I've mentioned, butterflies are creatures with a powerful and sometimes spiritual meaning, most often symbolising transformation and rebirth. It was soon clear why they were appearing in this message.

The spirit lady's name was Gloria and she was looking to connect with her daughter. The minute I mentioned butterflies, a young woman in the middle of the theatre raised her arm in the air.

Her name was Louise. 'Do you recognise this?' I asked her.

'Yes, I think of my mother as a butterfly. We also used to buy each other things with butterflies on them,' Louise said.

It turned out she was wearing a brooch with a butterfly on it that night. 'I've carried on buying them since mum passed. They always remind me of her,' she added, touching the brooch.

I could tell that her mother had something very specific to say about a particular butterfly, however. She began showing me a baby and a nursery. I could see that it had images of butterflies everywhere. 'Your mother's also saying that she likes the butterfly wallpaper in the nursery,' I said.

This brought a big smile to Louise's face.

I continued, 'She says it's lovely to think of her granddaughter looking at them during the first few weeks and months.' It turned out that Louise had been pregnant when her mother had passed over. Her greatest regret was that Gloria had never seen her daughter, Charlotte, she told me.

'She's telling me that she has seen her,' I said, as my mind was now filled with the image of a single, white butterfly hovering over the baby's cot. 'Your mother is showing me that she gave you a sign of her presence. Yesterday morning. The sign came in the shape of a white butterfly that your daughter was looking at,' I added.

Louise's face turned pale at this. She began shaking and held the hand of a friend who had come along to the theatre with her.

'Is that something you can understand?' I asked her.

'Yes. I found a butterfly in my baby daughter's room yesterday morning,' she confirmed. There were a couple of audible gasps in the audience at this. 'I couldn't work out how it had got in there,' Louise went on. 'I'd opened the window a tiny bit because it was a lovely morning. But I'd been surprised to see it had squeezed through the gap.'

'Your mother is saying that your daughter had been watching the butterfly for a while before you came into the room. She is saying that she felt happy to see it.'

Louise nodded. 'Yes, I only went in there because I thought I should check on her. She wasn't crying or anything,' she said. 'In fact she was burbling away happily.'

It's not often that the spirit world comes through to explain the actual meaning of the signs it delivers. In the vast majority of cases, it is left to the recipient to understand and appreciate what they have been shown. In Louise's case, however, the meaning couldn't have been explained more clearly – or aptly.

Butterflies can be a sign of transformation and change but also of life going on. So it was in this case. I'd be prepared to bet that, when she grows up, baby Charlotte will treasure the sight of butterflies as much as her mother and grandmother have done.

Sign Language: Three Wishes

If you are asking for a sign it has to be for a good reason. Don't waste the spirits' energy; make it something that is important. For instance, don't ask every five minutes, 'Shall I buy this dress, shall I buy these shoes?' Don't take it to the extreme.

I had a lady who came to me for a reading once. She wanted me to ask for a sign whether she should have another reading. I told her I wasn't going to waste my energy and – more importantly – I wasn't going to waste the energy of someone in the spirit domain. She had to work that out for herself.

The best comparison I can make is this: imagine you have three wishes. Would you waste those wishes on issues that you could solve yourself? Instead, use those wishes to deal with things that are important to you. Things that are life-changing, rather than things that are silly.

6 | Guidance and Godincidences

I sometimes see myself as someone who is in a boat with no oars. I could drift in any direction but I know that the signs and messages I get from the spirit world will guide me in the right direction. They are my winds and my tides. I really believe that.

I trust that they will bring the right people into my life. And I have faith that they will steer me to the places I need to be. If things are fine in my career and in my spiritual life they will go quiet. But if not, then they will intervene. They will even put blocks in front of me if I am not meant to do certain things.

The same forces are at work in all our lives. We are all shown signs and given spiritual nudges that are intended to move us in a certain direction. Sometimes these will be delivered by spirits that have taken physical form, events that I refer to as 'godincidences'. At other times, events will simply be manipulated to steer us in a certain direction. I have experienced both of these things myself and have heard many stories of others being guided by them too.

The Angel of the West

One of the most extraordinary types of signs that the spirit world can give us are known as 'godincidences'. These are very strong, visual presences that show themselves to us in order to directly influence events. For this reason they can be quite dramatic signs. Sometimes they have to be – in many cases, they can even represent the difference between life and death.

The most vivid example of this that I have experienced personally happened when I was driving to the West Country to see a friend a few years ago. I had just passed Bristol and was driving up a hill. I was travelling quite quickly, close to the 70 mph speed limit. I was, as I usually do, listening to music as I drove.

All of a sudden, I was transfixed by a figure standing at the side of the road. It was a man. He was about six foot tall and dressed from head to toe in black.

He was standing in a really odd place, on the grass just off the hard shoulder. There seemed to be no obvious reason why he was there. He wasn't standing by a broken-down car and he wasn't on the telephone to someone. He just seemed to be standing there, observing the world. It was very strange and it really threw me.

I found myself slowing down and slipping into the inside lane. I looked back at him a few times in the rear-view mirror. He remained fixed to the spot, not moving. Who on earth was he? And what was he doing simply standing by the side of the motorway like that? All sorts of thoughts began racing through my mind. For a moment, I even considered coming to a stop and going back to talk to him.

The moment had soon passed, however, and he began to slip out of view in the mirror. I had reached the brow of the hill.

All of a sudden I had to hammer on my brakes. In front of me all I could see was a wall of traffic. The entire motorway had come to a sudden, grinding halt.

I only just managed to come to a stop behind a lorry that was directly ahead of me. Other cars were skidding to a halt as well and I could see black tyre marks on the outside lane and smell burning rubber. Just ahead of me one car had clearly come to a really dramatic halt and was skewed across the road. Fortunately, however, none of the cars had hit each other with any real force. It could, quite easily, have been a major pile-up. People could have been badly hurt – even killed.

It was only later that it struck me what had happened. The man at the side of the road had clearly been a sign. If it hadn't been for him, I would have reached the brow of the hill travelling at 70 mph. If I had done so, I have no doubt that I would have ploughed into the traffic in front of me.

The fact that others managed to come to a halt suggests to me that the man must have distracted and slowed down others as well. He may well have saved many lives.

I remembered him quite recently when I was driving north up to Scotland and passed Antony Gormley's famous sculpture, *Angel of the North*, just outside Gateshead. There is something calming and protective about the giant metallic angel. He too slows people down and guides them safely on their way.

There is no doubt in my mind that what I witnessed that day years earlier in the West Country was something similar. When I think back on it now I refer to him as 'The Angel of the West'.

I may well owe him my life.

The Spiritual Satnav

The incident on the motorway was not the last time I found the spirit world offering me a sign that I should take a particular direction in my life. A few years ago, as I began to build a name for myself touring the country as a platform medium, I was asked to perform at a demonstration in Maidstone in Kent.

At that point in my career I used to get quite nervous in advance of public performances. But as the day of this demonstration drew near I was actually looking forward to it. I'd telephoned the organiser earlier in the week and he'd told me that it was a complete sell-out. I'd worked in the Kent area before and found audiences there to be very responsive and respectful.

At the time I was living in the cottage I'd found in the Essex countryside, not far from Stansted. Getting to Maidstone should have been a relatively easy task. I was within a few minutes' drive of the M11 motorway, from where I could take the M25 around London and then drop down into Kent. In all, the journey should have taken me an hour and a half at most.

With my son, James, and a friend of his, I set off with plenty of time to spare. It was late afternoon as we left home. We were scheduled to arrive a good hour before the demonstration began.

The drive to the motorway from our home takes a quarter of an hour. But when I hit the motorway I realised I was going to have a problem. As we arrived on the slip road to join the motorway we could see that the entire M11 was crammed full of cars. The point where we joined was quite elevated, so we had a good view of the country-side around us. We could see that the queue stretched for miles, bumper to bumper. It was complete gridlock.

We checked on the radio and the news confirmed our worst fears. For reasons that weren't yet quite clear, the motorway had ground to a halt. Nothing was moving in the clockwise direction that we wanted to head in. And it was little better in the opposite direction.

I began to panic. I hate letting people down, especially the sort of honest, decent and spiritual people who tend to come to my demonstrations. Other mediums were going to be present, too, and would be able to get the demonstration under way. But I already had visions of people sitting in an empty hall, muttering under their breath about how unreliable and unprofessional I was. I was already wondering whether it would kill my new career stone dead before it had really got going.

We sat in the traffic for the best part of an hour and in that time we moved no more than half a mile. I was begin-ning to despair. Every bulletin on the radio was warning drivers who weren't already stuck on the motorway to avoid the M11 and M25 at all costs. 'If you've got any sense, stay at home this evening,' one DJ said.

Every now and again we would nudge forward a hundred yards or so. But no sooner had we picked up any momentum than we ground to a halt again. It was unbearable. I was just getting to the point where I was ready to scream when a roundabout loomed into view. James and I had a quick exchange of views. We were in agreement that we should get off the road and see how the landscape looked from the roundabout.

Even achieving this short journey took us what seemed like an eternity. And when we reached the roundabout it was even worse than we'd thought. Traffic was now backed up not just on the motorway but on the road leading onto it too. And it was the same in both directions. Even if I'd wanted to turn round and go home, I wouldn't have been able to do so. I was going nowhere.

The roundabout had a turning for a service station and a restaurant. James and I agreed that we might as well head there for a cup of coffee and a rethink of our strategy. It would also give me a chance to make the difficult phone call I could already sense I would need to make to the organiser of the demonstration.

We decided to have a quick bite to eat and a drink, first. I figured that whatever happened, we weren't going to get a meal this evening otherwise. Eventually I reached the moment at which I had to make a decision.

James went out to listen to the car radio and the traffic

bulletins were still telling a tale of woe. Huge logjams all along the M25. Apparently the problem was related to a couple of major accidents. When he got back to me, he gave me a simple thumbs-down.

It was now less than an hour before the demonstration was due to start. Even if I could get going again, I was not going to get there in time – even if the motorway had been completely empty. I picked up the phone and rang the Maidstone number.

The gentleman who had organised the demonstration was very understanding about it. In fact, he said he'd suspected I might have a problem. He'd spoken to someone else who was trying to travel in the same direction and knew about the gridlock. 'Don't worry about it. We have someone else here who can do a small demonstration. We will see you next time,' he said.

I was extremely grateful for his patience. I promised to come down another time and told him to contact me with potential dates the following morning. I must admit I breathed a huge sigh of relief when I ended the call. It was a huge weight off my shoulders to have made the decision. I could almost feel my blood pressure subsiding.

We got back into the car and left the service station about twenty minutes later. The service station was tucked away off the motorway so you couldn't see the main roads until you had travelled about half a mile. As we drove along an empty road I kept expecting to see the rear end of a car looming into view as we rejoined the traffic jam. But there was nothing.

We made it all the way to the road back to Stansted encountering virtually no traffic. After a while we got a glimpse of the motorway and all you could see was traffic moving smoothly and swiftly in both directions.

I twiddled with the radio to find another travel bulletin. It seemed like the road problems had gone from being the only subject on the talk shows and phone-ins to a non-existent story.

Eventually a news bulletin announced that the problems on the M25 were now over. It seemed it had cleared really quickly about half an hour earlier. We were home within fifteen minutes.

Part of me was upset at what had happened. We had all become extremely stressed and worked up for nothing. And a lot of people would have been disappointed not to see me demonstrate. I slept a little uneasily that night. Deep down, however, something was telling me that what had happened would turn out to be for the best.

It was a couple of nights later, at the regular Wednesday night circle that I attended, that one of the circle members mentioned something they'd read on the internet.

A particular website – which shall remain nameless, I don't want to give them the benefit of any free publicity – had written something about me the previous day. This website was notorious among psychics and mediums for rubbishing everything and anything that we did. Their favourite tactic was to send someone along to sit in the audience during a demonstration, get them to secretly record what went on, then carefully to cherry pick the bits that they could use to 'prove' that what we did was completely bogus.

Some of the 'reports' they had published were extremely offensive and damaging. One or two mediums I'd met had talked about trying to sue them. But then someone had discovered that they were funded by a porn site, which meant that they were probably extremely well-off and it would have been extremely hard to bring an action against them, especially considering the nature of their so-called journalism. In general, psychics and mediums don't really stand much of a chance in a court of law.

The circle members said that the website had described how they had sent a 'reporter' to the Maidstone demonstration. In very sarcastic and scathing tones, the website feature had suggested that perhaps I'd got wind of the reporter's presence and 'chickened out' of appearing.

Hearing this really threw me for a moment. I didn't like the idea of this website targeting me. I had nothing to hide, far from it. I was proud of the work I was doing and would have defended it to anyone and everyone. But this website wasn't interested in hearing my point of view. They were just interested in making fun of and 'exposing' what they regarded as a less than respectable trade.

For a while I felt a mixture of emotions swirling around inside me. A small part of me was rather sorry that I hadn't been there to fight my corner. Another, larger part of me, however, was telling itself that – just as I'd suspected – it had been a good thing that I hadn't made it down to Maidstone that evening.

It was only later that night that it began to dawn on me what had happened a couple of evenings ago. I had been given a sign. The spirit world really hadn't wanted me to go to Maidstone. And they had somehow contrived to make sure I didn't get there.

Looking back on it now, I can see clearly why they had made this decision. Back then I was a relative newcomer to platform mediumship. My confidence was growing but it was still fragile. Years of self-doubt had been stripped away but it could very easily have returned if I'd been subjected to public ridicule. I might very easily have quit. The last thing I needed at that stage of my career was to have been the subject of a report by this website.

Instead, the spirit world had protected me. They had shown me a sign that had taken me off that road.

Now, I am not saying that the spirit world created a giant traffic jam on the M25 just to protect me from a website. That would be absurd. But what I am saying is that, by offering me a route off that motorway at that precise moment, the spirit world was acting in my best interests.

If I'd stayed on that motorway for another three quarters of an hour to an hour I might well have begun moving with the flow. I might even have been able to make the latter stages of the demonstration in Maidstone. If I'd done so, and if I'd been subjected to unkind and scathing reporting, I really do wonder whether I'd have carried on with my mediumship.

If this had been a one-off occurrence then I might have

questioned it. But it wasn't. It was one of many such moments, each of which has led me a little further down the particular road that I am following today.

That evening the spirit world acted as my spiritual satnav once more. By offering me the right sign they steered me away from trouble. I have a feeling I will be eternally grateful for that.

Down Memory Lane

There have been several other occasions when I've experienced the spirit world's guiding hand at work in my life. One that always sticks in my mind happened during an evening when I was away from home, touring and performing around the country.

I had given a demonstration at a theatre in High Wycombe and was heading off early to the West Country the following morning so I had booked into a hotel for the night. That evening, I was making my way after the show to the hotel with my friend Lucy, who had kindly agreed to drive me and keep me company on my tour.

She was using her satnav system to guide us and it should have been a relatively short drive back to the hotel. To be honest, I was shattered and was dying to get off to bed. I stretched myself out across the back seat and was soon half asleep as Lucy drove through the night.

After we'd been travelling for about a quarter of an hour or so, however, I was pulled out of my rather pleasant dreams by the sound of Lucy's voice. The car's indicators were ticking loudly and we'd pulled over on the side of the road. Lucy was leaning into the back of the car with a concerned look on her face. 'Sorry about this, Tracy, but I think we're a bit lost,' she said, apologetically.

'What do you mean? Everyone said it was only fifteen minutes' drive away. I thought it was easy to get to the hotel,' I mumbled.

'So did I, but the satnav seems to have gone bonkers and we've ended up heading in another direction completely.'

For a moment or two we just laughed. Fortunately we had enough petrol in the car and we both had our mobile phones on us.

'If the worst came to the worst we could pretend to break down and call the AA,' Lucy joked.

We were still howling with laughter as she put the car into gear again and headed off into the darkness once more. As she did so I tried to get myself back to sleep.

'Oh, here we go, we are entering a town. There should be some signs here. Or we can ask a local,' Lucy said, after what must have been five more minutes.

From my position stretched out in the back seat I couldn't see too clearly out of the car. 'What's the town called?' I asked for some reason, although, truth be told, I didn't much care.

Lucy's reply soon snapped me out of my sleepy state, however. 'Somewhere called Princes Risborough,' she said.

I was soon sitting bolt upright on the back seat. I had once known this part of the world quite well when I had been in a relationship with a guy who lived nearby. Princes Risborough had been the town in which we'd conducted most of our courtship. It was funny, but I'd been rushing around so much that I hadn't realised we were so close to it.

As I looked out into the dark night, only a few street-lights illuminating the town, I immediately recognised a building. It was an office block with a large gate outside it. The guy I'd been seeing used to work there. I remembered how, when I'd been up in the area once, I'd met him at the gates before heading out after work for a drink.

There was no one on the streets to guide us so we kept on driving for a bit. We'd soon come to a halt at a set of traffic lights. I looked across the road and saw a pub, lit up with Christmas lights. It looked like a party was going on inside.

'I don't believe it,' I said out loud.

'What?' Lucy asked.

'That's the pub I used to go to with this guy from around here. In fact, I can remember going to a party there,' I said. My mind flashed back to a night about twelve months earlier when we'd celebrated his birthday there. 'This is beginning to get a bit weird,' I said to myself, by now wide awake.

We were still unsure which direction to take to get back to our hotel. There seemed to be no major junctions with road signs to other towns. So we carried on with what was now turning into a bit of a magical mystery tour.

For the next couple of minutes it was as if I'd travelled back a year or so in time. I was literally driving down Memory Lane. Every turn we took, every street we went around contained little reminders of the time I'd spent with this guy. They were, it had to be said, happy times. We'd parted on relatively good terms. However, the pressure of my work combined with the fact that we'd lived so far away from each other had meant it hadn't been a relationship we could realistically pursue.

Eventually Lucy and I saw a road sign directing us towards the road we needed to take to our hotel. Lucy in particular breathed a sigh of relief. No more than ten minutes later, we pulled into the hotel driveway.

As happens so often when I'm touring, I had let someone else book the hotel and hadn't taken any notice of the details. In fact I don't think I'd even looked at the name. So, as Lucy steered us into the car park, and we clambered out to fish out our overnight bags from the boot of the car, it didn't occur to me that this place too might have been a reminder of the past.

I don't know why I was so surprised when I started walking towards the hotel entrance and saw the familiar, brightly-lit building. 'Oh my God,' I said to Lucy. 'This is where we used to stay when we were dating. He used to bring me here all the time!'

Rather than heading for my bed, I headed straight for the bar where Lucy and I both ordered a stiff drink. As we sat down and relaxed finally, I looked around a room that had, for a brief period, been as familiar as my own living room. It was only then that it dawned on me that this must be the work of the spirit world.

'There's obviously something going on here,' I said to Lucy.

'What do you mean?' she asked.

'Well I'm pretty sure the spirit world was responsible for us getting lost tonight. And I'm pretty sure that they were in control of the satnav that sent us into Princes Risborough.'

'OK. So what does that mean?' Lucy wondered, looking perplexed.

'Well, my guess is that it means the guy I used to see from around here is about to come into my life again. Which is odd, given that I haven't heard a word from him for the past twelve months at least.'

I knew that the guy had left the area quite soon after we'd ended our relationship. He'd worked in Scotland for a while but, given the nature of his job, could have been working in Timbuktu by now as far as I knew. A small part of me wondered whether he was going to suddenly walk into the bar and tell me he too was here on business.

But I didn't hang around long enough to find out. I was by now far too tired.

Lucy and I finished our drinks and headed up to the warmth of our rooms. After a quick shower, I tucked myself up in my bed and plugged my mobile phone charger into the socket next to me.

It was then that I noticed I had a text message from about five minutes earlier. I must have missed it while I was in the shower.

My eyes nearly jumped out of my head when I read who it was from. It was the guy I'd been dating here a year ago.

The message simply said: 'Are you thinking about me?'

The Guardian Angel

A while ago, I was introduced to a lady named Fiona who had been disabled by a degenerative illness, which had made it very hard for her to walk. Fiona lived in a village just north of London and was married to a lovely guy, Tom, who had looked after her brilliantly ever since her disability had struck when she was in her thirties.

Her life had been turned upside down completely when Tom contracted a serious illness and was admitted to a hospital in central London. He was confined to a bed there for several weeks and many of her friends feared for Fiona's welfare during this time. She had been forced to fend for herself, something she hadn't done for a long time. But she had proven herself a resilient lady and coped well. And she had been absolutely devoted in visiting her husband as often as she possibly could.

This wasn't easy, mind you. Fiona had a specially converted car but couldn't drive to the hospital because car parking was difficult even for someone with a disabled parking badge. The first time she'd tried, she'd ended up in a car park so far away from the hospital entrance that she'd almost collapsed with exhaustion by the time she got to the ward in which Tom was a patient.

She was lucky in the sense that she had some very helpful friends who would drive her to the hospital. But, as so often happens with long-term illness, as time went on, she found herself forced more and more to get there by herself, using public transport.

She wasn't someone who usually went on trains and

tubes so she'd initially been very nervous about travelling. Because she was disabled, Fiona had to plan the journey very carefully, making sure the stations she changed at didn't have long flights of stairs. She also had to allow lots of time to get there during the strict visiting hours.

To her credit she managed the trip several times. After a while, however, the strain began to take its toll. And one day the inevitable happened.

Towards the end of a journey that had been more stressful than usual, she nodded off briefly. She woke up with a start, to see her train pulling into her stop sooner than she had anticipated. It usually took her a while to get herself out of her seat so she immediately became worried that she wouldn't be able to make it off the train before the doors slid closed.

The carriage was virtually empty and no one was sitting near her so she wasn't able to ask anyone for help. In her rush to get out, she panicked and stumbled to the floor. Her condition meant she couldn't easily get up again. She would have to crawl along and haul herself up on to a seat. For some reason the train doors remained open for a while. But – overcome with a mixture of exhaustion and embarrassment – she resigned herself to lying on the floor until she found the energy to haul herself up or someone else lifted her. In the middle of the day, however, there seemed little prospect of that happening on an empty train. And then something very strange happened.

The carriage had been eerily quiet. She assumed this was because the few passengers who were on board had all got off. But then, completely out of the blue, she felt herself being picked up from behind by a pair of strong arms. Not only did the hands lift her up, they then guided her off the train with all her belongings before safely depositing her on to the platform, where she was able to regain her composure.

The person helping her didn't say a word during all this. Fiona had kept saying 'thank you' but received no reply. Once she was safely on her feet on the platform, she turned round to thank her knight in shining armour. She had already formed an image in her mind of him. He must have been a six-foot-tall male, probably in his twenties or thirties.

But there was no one there. The station platform was as empty as the carriage from which she'd just emerged. For a moment Fiona thought she'd gone mad. Clearly someone had lifted her off the carriage floor and on to the platform. She was pretty certain it was a man. But she couldn't hear any footsteps disappearing down the labyrinth of station tunnels. And there was no one in the carriage at all.

What had happened? Who was her saviour and where did he come from? Was he from this physical world or was he perhaps from the spirit world? Fiona was in a complete state of shock for a little while.

Of course, she didn't tell her husband about any of this when she finally got to his bedside that day. By now he was making a good, but slow, recovery. She didn't want him to worry about her any more than he already was.

It was only when she got home that night that she rang a friend. She was dying to tell someone about her strange experience. The friend was someone who had a strong belief in the spirit world and its power to come to our aid at times of dire need. She wasted no time at all in telling Fiona what she thought had happened. 'It was your guardian angel,' she said.

Fiona was something of a fence-sitter when it came to the idea of an afterlife and spirits. So she just laughed at first. 'Yes, of course, but I didn't see any wings flapping at his side,' she giggled.

She didn't regard it as a joke for long, however. The friend brought her a book about strange spirit and psychic phenomena, which included several accounts from around the world which were remarkably similar to Fiona's experience. She read how other people had found themselves lying in distress in disaster zones, in the middle of military battles or just alone in the middle of nowhere, when someone or something had come to their aid. In each case, the rescuer never made him- or herself known to the person being rescued and had disappeared into thin air the instant the rescued one was safe.

I first met Fiona some time after the event when we were introduced by the friend who had bought her the book. Fiona knew what I did for a living and wasted no time in asking me what I thought about what had happened to her. I said I agreed with our mutual friend. Apparently, she now routinely refers to the 'day she was rescued by her guardian angel'.

A Helping Hand

My belief in the power of signs isn't unique. I have many friends who have experienced moments where their lives have been touched or influenced by the spirit world. Some have encountered situations where they are convinced the spirit world's intervention has made a life-or-death difference. In some families, the experience almost seems to be something that is passed down through the generations.

That certainly seemed to be the case with a friend of mine, a lovely lady called Mariayolanda. With a name like that you won't be surprised to discover that her family originally comes from Italy – Sicily, to be precise. She is convinced that she and her Sicilian family are guided and helped out by the spirit world. The more I hear of her family's experiences, the more convinced I am that she is right.

The family tradition seems to have begun many years ago when Mariayolanda's maternal grandparents emigrated to London sometime after the Second World War. Her grandfather didn't really take to life in England. Almost from the beginning, he had insisted that it was only a short-term measure and that he would one day return to Sicily. He didn't feel he could make a real living in Britain.

Her grandmother, however, didn't want to go back to the island. In Sicily they had suffered nothing but bad luck, as far as she was concerned. She saw no reason to return and was convinced it would only bring them more ill fortune. She believed that if they were going to build a better life for their children and grandchildren, they needed to stay in England.

After a few years, however, their dream of a new life was fading and even she had had to admit it wasn't working out. Both of them were working hard in regular jobs but they couldn't seem to get ahead. Finally, the grandfather became despondent and said he wanted to go back to Sicily.

No matter what his wife said, he couldn't be dissuaded. One morning, before he headed off to work, he told his wife that he was going to start making arrangements to pack up all their belongings, deal with all their loose ends in London and head back to Palermo in Sicily. His wife felt terribly sad about this but – grudgingly – accepted it.

That day, her husband set off for work early. She was about to leave the house to head to her job when she smelled something burning.

There was no sign of anything amiss in the kitchen, but when she ran into the hallway she saw smoke coming from a cupboard under the stairs. When she threw it open she discovered that some coats had somehow burst into flames. She had absolutely no idea how this could have happened but didn't have time to dwell on it anyway. Instead, she immediately ran to the kitchen, grabbed a pail of water and dampened the fire.

The fire really shook her. She couldn't help thinking what might have happened if she hadn't got there at that precise moment. Another five minutes and the whole house might have gone up in flames. And she couldn't for the life of her work out how it had started. It was a mystery.

The fire was only the beginning of a string of unfortunate events that were to unfold that day. On the way to work, she almost got run over. She was probably still distressed by the fire in her home and wasn't concentrating when she stepped into a busy street. There was a loud blaring of a horn and a screech of tyres. She missed being hit by a speeding car by a matter of inches.

By the time she got to work she was emotionally drained. Even worse was to come, however. She worked at a large factory in London, cutting fabric. That afternoon at work, one of the machines malfunctioned and came down on top of her hands. She let out the most almighty scream. There was blood everywhere and she was in absolute agony. When her colleagues got to her, they saw that two of her fingers had been severed.

She was rushed to hospital, but there was nothing the doctors could do to save the fingers. The kind of surgery we take for granted today didn't even exist then.

The accident was entirely her employers' fault. The factory was forced to pay her handsome compensation, hundreds of pounds, which back then was a life-changing amount of money.

While his wife was recovering from the accident, her husband postponed his plans to go back to Italy. When they received news of the compensation payment, he abandoned them altogether and decided they would remain in England.

Money – or, to be more precise, a lack of it – had been a factor in the grandfather's decision to go back to Sicily. He wanted to run his own business but simply didn't have the funds to do so in England. Now he did. And so they decided to stay in London.

Together, they launched a business that became very successful. It was the first of many that made their fortune. They did eventually return to Sicily many times, but only on family holidays when they visited relatives in the 'old country'.

Mariayolanda's grandmother always maintained that the spirit world had played a part in deciding their fate. She was convinced that the incidents that day were signs. How else could she have had three very different life-threatening experiences in the space of a few hours? She was also adamant that it was the moment that changed her life around. Somewhere, someone had a plan for her and her husband. She had had to go through a lot of pain to get there. But she did.

The other strange story involved Mariayolanda herself. One summer, she was in Sicily visiting her relatives, and driving along a particularly beautiful coastal road in an open-top sports car with her female cousins. She was young at the time and they were all in high spirits. As she put it to me when she told me the story, she had the stereo turned up, and she and her cousins were on the lookout for any good-looking boys.

I know from personal experience that Mariayolanda usually likes to drive pretty fast. She knew the roads in Sicily well and as she was driving a fast car, she would normally have been flying along with the wind in her hair. But on this particular day something odd happened. She found that she couldn't accelerate.

'I just couldn't press the pedal down; it was like there was a brick under it,' she explained to me.

Mariayolanda is a great believer in the power of the spirit realm. So when she heard a voice in her head telling her to 'leave it, don't force it,' she did just that. She took it easy. She was having a great time anyway, so driving a little slower than usual was no great sacrifice.

Moments later, she swung the car around a particularly tight blind corner in the middle of a coastal village. The instant she emerged around the corner she had to hammer on the brakes, drawing screams from her cousins.

A toddler, a little boy, had ridden his tiny tricycle right out into the road, in front of their car. If Mariayolanda had been travelling five or ten miles an hour faster, she would without doubt have hit the little child and probably killed him.

Mariayolanda was momentarily shaken by the close shave. 'I stopped just in time. If I had hit that child at the speed I would normally have been driving, he would never have survived and I'd never have forgiven myself,' she told me years later.

Today, Mariayolanda is convinced she got not one but two signs telling her to cut her speed in advance of turning around that blind bend in Sicily. The first came in the shape of the accelerator pedal. The second came in the form of the voice she heard in her head.

She is convinced that the same forces which influenced her grandparents' lives so dramatically had intervened once again.

Moments like this continued to occur within the family. Many years later, Mariayolanda's grandfather had a stroke in the middle of a heart by-pass operation. He was in a coma for three months.

The hospital authorities kept predicting the worst. At one point the surgeon spoke to Mariayolanda's nan, mum and aunties, to prepare them for the worst. The doctor said it might even be a blessing in disguise. If he emerged from his coma, Granddad might not be able to walk or talk again. However, the doctor's advice divided the family.

Mariayolanda's mother said she didn't believe the medical advice. 'He will come out of this and he will be fine,' she said.

Her aunties, on the other hand, said they should listen to the professionals. The women ended up having a shouting match. 'Didn't you hear what the doctor said?' the aunties shouted at her mum.

'He isn't God!' her mother responded.

That night Mariayolanda's mother had a vivid dream. In it, her father appeared and asked for a glass of water and a plate of pastina, the 'baby pasta' which Italian mothers feed sickly members of the family.

The following day she visited her father on her own. As she sat by his bedside, he woke up and immediately asked her for a glass of water and a plate of pastina.

Overjoyed, Mariayolanda's mum ran down the corridors, trying to find a nurse or doctor. She found the doctor who had delivered the bad news the previous day. When she explained what she'd heard he looked sceptical. He told her she must have imagined it. Her father was in a deep coma and was unlikely to emerge from it just like that.

But nevertheless he went back to the room with her to see her father, who he found sitting upright in bed. 'Hello, sir,' her father said. Apparently the doctor nearly collapsed from shock.

Sadly, Mariayolanda's grandfather didn't live for much longer. He contracted pneumonia and passed away. His family were soon feeling his presence in their lives again, however.

His wife had always joked with him that, when he returned to see her after he had passed, he would do so in the shape of a wasp or a fly. So when bugs began appearing in an unusual way soon after his passing, she took notice.

It was winter and there really shouldn't have been any bugs in the first place. But every now and again they saw one, hovering near where the family gathered. When one particularly large, fat fly appeared in late December, Mariayolanda's mother exchanged knowing looks with her sisters, who were visiting. 'Look, Dad has come to say hi and check that we are all right,' she smiled.

There were other signs of the old man's presence. He used to smoke quite heavily until shortly before he died. In the weeks after his passing, Mariayolanda and other family members could smell tobacco smoke in the kitchen. No one else in the family smoked and in fact no one was allowed to light up in the house.

The most striking sign, however, came when Mariayolanda took a photograph of her own father. When she blew it up she found two orbs hovering over him, one near his leg and another one over his heart. (Chapter 9 explains the amazing phenomenon of orbs in more detail.) When the images were blown up even more, the family became convinced there was an image of their grandfather in there. And they became even more convinced of his presence in the weeks that followed.

First, Mariayolanda's father was told he needed a knee replacement on the leg that the orb had been hovering over. Then, within just a few weeks of that, he was rushed into hospital with a heart problem. He nearly died and needed a quadruple heart by-pass.

I was shown the photos before this happened and at the time I predicted that something of the kind was going to happen. But their granddad's presence had also told me that everything was going to be all right. In fact, with him around to watch over them, they were always going to be all right . . .

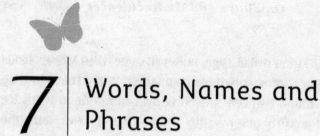

7 | Words, Names and Phrases

One of the simplest and most common ways in which the spirit world makes its presence felt is by placing names, words or phrases in front of us. They may appear in all sorts of ways – in books, newspapers or magazines most obviously, but also on advertising hoardings and street signs, in text messages and even on car numberplates.

Since I became a medium I have heard of many cases in which names or words have helped people connect to the spirit world around them. In some cases these signs have even guided them towards important decisions or offered an insight into something significant in their lives.

Love Is All Around

When I am not demonstrating mediumship in theatres I spend most of my time working at the Dragonfly Centre, a meeting place for psychics, mediums and all those interested in the spirit world, which I run in the ancient town of Waltham Abbey, northeast of London. One of the great pleasures of running this place is that I can provide other mediums and psychics with a home in which to develop their talents. Today all sorts of classes are run there – not just on mediumship but also other psychic phenomena. It is wonderful to watch people growing in this environment.

I can't provide a platform for every medium in the country, however. I also have to protect the reputation my centre has won for its openness and high standards. So I have to be selective about those whom I allow to work there. Often, I rely on the spirit world to guide me in making some of these decisions.

An example of this occurred quite recently. I had been approached by a medium called Jay Love who wanted to teach a class in the centre. I knew of him. He had a good reputation both as a medium and a person. When he'd been sixteen he had been told by a medium that he would one day work for the spirit world. He had come through some rough times, including the death of his parents, and had established himself as one of the brightest young talents around. He'd spoken to me about what he wanted to do at the centre and I'd been impressed. I had been inclined to say yes and invite him to work with us.

Before doing this, however, I decided to put out a request to the spirit world. It is very important to me that I maintain the right atmosphere in the centre. I didn't want to get this decision wrong and introduce someone who would somehow affect the equilibrium and peace of the place. I asked the spirit world to give me some sort of sign that I was doing the right thing.

That evening, I sat with my regular Wednesday night circle. The people within the group include some very close friends, people whom I trust totally. We meet at a very specific time and I insist that no one can arrive late. Once the circle is formed, that is it. No one else can join in that evening.

I noticed that one of the chairs was empty. It was usually occupied by a lady called Pam. She was normally extremely punctual, so I assumed something was wrong. I also knew that she had to travel from her home in the country and had to negotiate some narrow lanes to get to us.

I went downstairs to wait for her and – sure enough – she appeared, looking flustered and slightly out of breath. 'Sorry I'm late, Tracy,' she said. 'Got stuck behind this woman driving this great big four by four. She was travelling about five miles an hour and holding everybody up. There was no way I could get past her.'

'That's OK,' I said.

Pam soon calmed down and we began making our way into the room where our circle sat. As we were climbing the stairs, Pam started laughing. 'The funny thing about this car was the numberplate,' she said. 'It was J LUV. I can tell you I didn't love it very much while I was stuck behind it.'

I did a double take. 'Sorry, Pam, what did you say?'

'The numberplate was J LUV. It was probably 1 LUV originally but this woman had got them to make the 1 look like a J. Must mean something, I suppose,' she said, taking her seat.

It almost certainly did mean something to whoever was driving the four by four. But it meant even more to me.

The fact that it was connected to what had been a negative moment for Pam didn't bother me. That was what the spirits had needed to do in this instance. How else would Pam have remembered the numberplate? It was a sign from the spirit world, of that there was no doubt.

'Thanks very much, Pam. You've made my mind up about something that's been bugging me,' I said.

'Really?' she said, looking puzzled.

'I will tell you about it sometime,' I said, aware that we really needed to get on with the circle.

The next morning I rang Jay Love and told him that I would be delighted for him to start teaching at my centre. He did very well and was soon a valuable addition to the team working there. The spirit world had helped me make a good decision.

I love it when that happens!

A Van on the Motorway

A friend of mine, Paul, was at an important crossroads in his life. He was a talented healer but lacked the confidence to really follow his gift. I was encouraging him to start his own circle but he kept saying he wasn't sure if he was ready. The turning point came one day after we'd had a long chat. Once again I'd told him that he should go for it and start his own healing circle. He was driving home when two things happened almost immediately.

The first piece of music Paul heard on his car radio was the song 'Tracy' by the 1980s group Level 42. The song had barely finished playing when he was cut up by a van on the M25. The white van had a company logo on it. It was Higgs.

He rang me that night to tell me about it. He also told me that he had decided to take the plunge and start a circle.

He reminded me of this incident recently. 'Coincidence? I think not,' he laughed.

The Psychic Estate Agent

Moving home is always a big decision. Finding the right place can be a long-drawn-out and stressful business. So when the time came for me to move out of the cottage I had been renting near Stansted so that I could rent a much larger house I was grateful for all the advice I could get. As usual, this meant getting not just the advice of estate agents but asking for the guidance of the spirit world as well. And they didn't let me down.

When I'd first decided that my son, James, and I needed more space in which to live and work, I had gone to a local estate agent in the Waltham Abbey area. I wanted something with lots of room, but within easy reach of my centre.

I'd been offered all sorts of weird and wonderful places – none of which were remotely right for me. I was just beginning to get a bit down about our situation when I got a call from a good friend of mine, Scott. He told me he was moving to another property with his girlfriend but was in the fortunate position where he didn't need to sell his existing home. 'How do you fancy renting it off me, Tracy?' he'd said.

His offer threw me a little. I knew his house well. It was a great house, very large and roomy. It even had its own swimming pool. I also didn't have a problem at all with Scott being my landlord. I'd known him for years and we trusted each other.

My heart was saying 'yes' immediately and my head wasn't far off reaching the same decision. But before I made the final leap and accepted Scott's offer, however, I decided to put it out to the spirit world. If they gave me a sign that it was the right thing to do then I would go ahead. If they didn't, I would pass up the offer and continue looking with the estate agents.

I wanted James to like it too, so I arranged with Scott to take him on a tour of the house. He took an immediate liking to it. I could sense that he wanted me to go for it. But he also knew I needed final validation from spirit.

The evening after we'd viewed the house, I had to drive down to Catford in southeast London to give a demonstration that night. It was a long drive, all the way through London to an area that I didn't know that well, so James agreed to come with me.

All the way there, I was mulling over what to do about Scott's house. I'd promised him an answer by the following day because he was heading away on holiday and would need to put the legal process in motion if we were going to move in.

As we drove through north and central London and across the Thames into south London, James and I discussed the pros and cons. We weighed up what we'd be losing by leaving the cottage, against what we'd be gaining by moving into the bigger house. The argument wasn't quite as clear-cut as I'd thought it was. We'd been very happy in the cottage but at the same time we knew the time was right for a move.

As we arrived in the Catford area, I began looking for somewhere to park. We turned off into some side streets to follow a sign for a car park that we'd been told was within easy walking distance of the theatre where I was doing the demonstration in a couple of hours' time.

As we were driving I saw Stanley Road on the right. 'Oh, there's a good sign,' I said to James, referring to my granddad, Stanley. Anything with the word Stanley in it is always a good omen for me.

As we went up a hill we then turned into another road, St Mary's Road. This was exactly the same name as the road which Scott's house was in, way back up in north London. 'Hmmm, I think someone's trying to tell us something,' I said to James.

This, of course, wasn't anywhere near enough to give me a complete answer to the question I'd put out to the spirits. I couldn't go on two pieces of information like that. I needed something more substantial.

As we approached the entrance to the car park, we stopped at a set of traffic lights. Ahead to the right, dominating the street, was a giant advertising hoarding. James and I both looked at it, then looked back at each other with the same expression on our faces.

'I don't believe it,' I said, sounding like a female version of Victor Meldrew.

The advertising hoarding was devoted to an advert by a local estate agent named Scotts. The main headline, which was written in giant type across the middle of the hoarding, read simply: 'SCOTTS LETTING AGREED'.

A few minutes later, after we'd parked the car and started walking to the theatre, my phone went. It was Scott.

'If you are OK to go ahead I've sorted out a draft agreement,' he said. 'I can give you until the morning if you need it. I know it's a big decision.'

I told him about the advertising hoarding which I'd driven past and which James and I could still see looming over us in the distance.

'Oh, that's freaky,' Scott laughed.

'So, anyway, I think that means it has to be a yes,' I said.

Now, other people might have put that down to coincidence. Those three things could have cropped up anywhere. There are many, many Stanley Roads and probably just as many St Mary's Roads all around the country. Every street in London has advertising hoardings and many of them have estate agents' boards boasting that lettings had been agreed.

All that is true enough. But how many of them say 'Scotts Letting Agreed', and how many of them would have been staring me in the face on the day when I had asked the spirit world to help me reach a decision? I had never been wrong when I'd followed the signs in the past. And I was pretty sure I wasn't wrong now.

And so it proved. I still live in that house, as does James. We have both been extremely happy there.

You have to ask for help sometimes. If you don't, how can you expect the spirit world to know you need help?

Changing Lanes

A lot of people imagine that communications from the spirit world must be very complicated things. How else can they make the leap between the two dimensions?

The reality is different. Yet I'm not going to say that tuning in to the vibrations of the spirit dimension is easy. Signs and messages can be incredibly hard to decipher. In the case of messages, in particular, mediums have to spend many years learning how to properly and accurately channel the energy, and how to interpret correctly what is being communicated. In some ways it is like learning a new language. Some learn to speak it well; others become so fluent it could be their mother tongue.

But sometimes messages from the spirit realms are not very complicated at all. In fact, they can be the simplest things in the world. Sometimes their meaning can be staring you in the face. All you have to do is recognise them for what they are.

This is particularly true with signs. There have been times when the spirit world has placed the most obvious signs in front of me and yet I've completely failed to see them. I haven't been able to see what's right under my nose. A good example of this happened to me a few years ago when I was driving down the M4 to a show in the West Country. The traffic was terrible, really heavy and bumper-to-bumper for long stretches of motorway. As if that wasn't bad enough, the road was packed with large vans and lorries. I really don't like driving in traffic like that, especially as some van and lorry drivers can be such aggressive and unpredictable drivers. I can get really annoyed with them. They seem to have no concept of how dangerous their driving can be at times.

As I plodded my way down the M4 on this particular afternoon there was one van that was driving in a particularly irritating, not to mention reckless, way. I first noticed it soon after I joined the M4 on the other side of Heathrow, having come off the M25. The van had been in the inside lane but, perhaps spotting a gap, it just darted across into the middle and then the outside lane, forcing at least one car to jam on the brakes. It was a white van that looked like it belonged to a plumber. There was a name on it in big blue letters: Robinson.

Every now and again the van would veer from side to side, as if the driver had lost control. It would also go through spells when it would speed up, then slow down again. It was doing my head in, to be honest. I tried my best to shake it off. My car was much faster than the van, so I kept overtaking it. But because the traffic was so heavy, it kept reappearing, often sliding past to overtake me on the passenger's side.

After a while, it established a position one or two vehicles in front of me. So it was never really out of my sight. Every now and again it would pull out into the outside lane in front of me. At one point I found myself sounding my horn at it. It didn't make any difference. As we got further away from London the traffic died down a little, allowing me to put my foot to the pedal and get well ahead of the van. As I went by I looked across at the driver but couldn't really make out his features. All I could see, in fact, was an even bigger version of the sign on the back – Robinson, again in giant blue letters. For a while my brain was pounding with the word.

I'd just begun to put it to the back of my mind when I pulled in for petrol at a service station the other side of Swindon. By now my mind was beginning to focus on tonight's performance. I'd forgotten about the van. Back on the motorway, I'd barely travelled three miles when I saw something looming up in front of me. The traffic had thickened up once more and the middle lane had ground to a halt. There, sitting right in front of me at the back of the queue, was the same van with the same signage staring at me. Robinson.

It felt like I'd driven into a scene from the Steven Spielberg movie *Duel*, about a guy who finds himself pursued by a giant truck which he simply can't shake off. I resigned myself to staring at the back of the van for the rest of my time on the M4. Luckily that wasn't much longer.

I breathed a huge sigh of relief when my turning off the motorway appeared and I saw the van carry straight on past it towards the Severn Bridge. The rest of my drive to the theatre was uneventful – thank goodness.

However, that night's demonstration was a mixed bag, as such performances can often be. For some reason the energy in the hall wasn't great, which in turn affected my energy levels. At one point, I found myself really struggling to interpret the message I was getting from a man. He was a father, I could sense that. But I couldn't find anything else to go on. None of the evidence I was offering to the audience was being recognised. At one point I thought I had the man's name and offered him Rob or Robert, but it didn't connect. I could feel the audience getting a little restless.

It was then that inspiration arrived – in the most unlikely form. All of a sudden, my mind was full of speeding traffic. It was as if I was back on the M4. Then something familiar loomed into view. Flashing in and out of view in front of me, was that plumber's van and the single word in blue, staring out at me: Robinson. In an instant I saw what I was being shown. 'This is a message from a man called Robin,' I said. 'He wants to communicate with his son, who is here in the audience tonight.'

Immediately, I saw a hand being raised. It was a young man, probably in his twenties. His name was Gordon. He confirmed that his father's name was Robin. It was just the kick-start the reading needed. I went on to deliver the young man a very moving and detailed message from his father, who had passed in tragic circumstances, from cancer, a few months earlier.

As I drove to my hotel after the show that night the roads offered a stark contrast to the M4. They were virtually empty. Sometimes I forget how resourceful and clever the spirit world is in delivering me the signs I need in order to do my job. I forget that they actually want me to connect their dimension to this physical world and that they will actively go out of their way to guide me. Ordinarily I'd never have thought of the name 'Robin'. Fortunately, the spirit world had primed me.

I'd had instances of this happening before. I remember once when I was driving to my health club and I saw a yellow truck sign-painted with red writing saying 'Richardson'. As we went further along I saw another lorry painted with the name Thomas. For some reason, both names came together in my head. Richardson Thomas. Suddenly I thought of a friend of mine Richard, who has a son called Thomas. A few minutes later I understood what this meant and why I'd been shown it. I hadn't spoken to Richard in ages. As I climbed out of the car and walked across the health club car park, he rang me on my mobile. 'That's funny, I was just thinking about you,' I said.

Turning the Pages

It is perhaps not surprising that the spirit world often uses books to deliver a sign. After all, they are perhaps the most powerful sources of ideas that we possess in this world. Over the years I have heard many stories of signs that have been delivered in this way. Some have had a direct influence on my life and on those with whom I work.

When a lady called Fiona Faery walked into the famous Hughes & Hughes bookshop on Grafton Street in Dublin a few years ago, she was not just looking for a book – she was also searching for some direction in her life.

She had begun exploring her abilities as a psychic medium and was keen to learn more about the subject. However, she was really uncertain about what she was going to do with her gift. Deep down, a part of her wasn't even sure if she had one that was worth sharing with the rest of the world. She really was at a crossroads.

At first, the bookshop didn't provide many answers. As she ran her eye along the shelves stacked with books by famous past and present mediums – from Doris Stokes to Colin Fry – nothing in particular caught her eye. But then something odd happened. A book literally jumped out at her. It fell off one of the shelves and landed at her feet.

It was by me. It was a copy of my first book, *Living with the Gift.*

My name meant nothing to her at that point in her life. Why should it have? I was well known here in the UK for appearing as one of the *Three Mediums* and for my work on the TV series *Psychic Private Eyes* but I wasn't exactly a household name, certainly not in Ireland.

Nevertheless, Fiona couldn't ignore the fact that this book had landed at her feet. As she pored over the first few pages she realised that she had to read it. A voice in her head confirmed it. 'Buy this book,' it said.

It proved to be a good decision – both for her and for me.

Soon afterwards Fiona turned up at a residential workshop course I was running at a place called Buckland Hall in the Brecon Beacons in Wales. The course was designed to help people develop and improve their mediumship.

Fiona had worked at psychic fairs in Ireland but hadn't really done what is known as platform mediumship, where you stand up in front of an audience and deliver the messages that are being channelled through you by the spirit world. However, during the workshop I got Fiona to stand on a platform in front of a group of other students and try out her gift. To her delight – and mild amazement I think – it really worked. There was no doubt in my mind that she had a real talent, a genuine gift.

During the course of the workshop I got to know a bit more about her. She had a slight advantage in this respect as she'd read a book about me. But as we talked we realised we shared a great deal in common.

I told her that I had been in a very similar position to her a few years earlier. I too had discovered my gift late in life. Thanks to a group of really supportive people I had been able to develop and explore it.

I told her about the occasion when I was starting out and I had attended a similar course to this at the famous Arthur Findlay College, near Stansted in Essex. One of the teachers there had forced me to stand on a platform for the first time. I told Fiona how terrified I'd been, how unsure I'd been of my right to even be standing there. But, like her, I'd come through. And I'd discovered and developed my gift.

Most amazingly of all, however, I told her about an incident that I hadn't mentioned to anyone previously. It too involved a book. One day, during a break from tuition at the Arthur Findlay College, I had gone to the building's fabulous old library. Suddenly a book had just flown off the shelves and landed on the floor in front of me. It was called *White Feather* and it had been written by a Native American of the same name.

I opened it up on a random page. The first sentence I saw read simply: 'Tracey runs a circle.' They were four words that changed the course of my life.

It turned out that White Feather was my guide. Along with another spirit messenger, a former Irish potato farmer called Paddy, he was the one who led me through the early part of my development as a medium.

Until that point in my life I had thought of my mediumship mainly as a hobby. But after that extra-ordinary experience, I put renewed energy into my work.

As I told this story Fiona looked at me almost disbelievingly. 'I can't believe that so many things have happened to us that are so similar,' she said.

We both left the Brecon Beacons convinced that we had been fated to meet. The spirit world had engineered it so that our paths had crossed. There was a reason why we had been put together. All we needed to do was work out what that reason was – and to act upon it.

It didn't take long for us to work it out. We continued to speak and met at a couple of other courses and events. Again we got on well. I invited Fiona over to do readings at my own Dragonfly Centre in Waltham Abbey and elsewhere. Soon she was travelling over to England from Ireland on a regular basis.

By the end of 2009 we had formed something of a

double act. Today, I am about to invite her to appear as a guest on stage with me during my tours.

It had all started with a sign in a Dublin bookshop. Who knows, one day there might be a book written about the pair of us . . .

An Instrument of Spirit

I am very respectful of the spirit world. I count it as a huge privilege that I have been given the ability to connect with it more easily than most people. When I am unsure of the direction my work is taking, I often ask the spirit world for guidance and reassurance. Invariably, they provide it. And yet I am very careful about how I use my gift.

One of the most enjoyable things that my success as a professional psychic and medium has allowed me to do has been to branch into writing. It's not something that I'd ever imagined I'd be asked to do, but now not only do I write books like this, but I also contribute to magazines. When I do so, however, I always check with spirit.

There's a particular example of this that springs to mind. It involves one of the magazines I write for regularly, which is called *Fate & Fortune*. They usually give me a range of assignments, one of which is to look into famous and controversial cases from the past. It is, in many ways, an offshoot of my work on the TV series *Psychic Private Eyes*. I take a cold case and investigate it both psychically and mediumistically. I then report my results.

A while ago I was given an assignment to investigate the life of a man called Robert Johnson. I will be honest and admit that I didn't have a clue who he was. My son, James, was familiar with him, but I wasn't.

As I researched into his life I discovered why he holds such a fascination for people. Johnson was a poor, black man who grew up in Mississippi. He was, however, a gifted young musician who played a variety of instruments. It was when he took up the guitar in his late teens that his life changed. Johnson quickly established himself as one of the greatest blues players of all time and is regarded by people like Eric Clapton as one of the greatest guitar players ever.

A legend built itself around Johnson. It was claimed that he'd travelled to a crossroad at midnight where he'd met a large black man. The man had, in fact, been the devil. He had made a pact with Johnson that, in return for his tuning his guitar and giving him an instant ability to play it, Johnson would play the blues, the so-called devil's music.

And Johnson had agreed.

I felt really uneasy about this. Johnson himself had helped build the legend by not denying the story. Some claim it was for publicity purposes. Others claimed that he had come back from spirit, regretting what he'd done and talking of a hellish existence on the Other Side.

I wasn't sure that I should be delving into this man's life. When I work as a medium, spirits come to me of their own free will. I don't do the reverse – I don't head off into the spirit realm and seek out individuals. There is a big difference.

So I decided to put out a thought to the spirit world. I

asked: 'Is this the right thing for me to be doing?' I got an answer within minutes.

As you know, I have had many instances of books falling at my feet. This happened again: a book that had been perched on a coffee table flopped on to the carpet in front of me. The weird thing was it was a book that I didn't know I possessed. However, I was familiar with the book, *The Teachings of Silver Birch* as communicated through Maurice Barbanell. But I'd never read it and didn't know I had a copy in the house.

It turned out James had borrowed this copy from a friend but that was beside the point. It had landed at my feet for a reason.

I did what I often do with books and turned to a random page to see if there was a sign for me. Immediately, a passage jumped out at me. It talked about the fact that we are all instruments of spirit. It also encouraged everyone to follow their gift, to do what they have been put on this earth to do.

This chimed with something that I'd long felt. The word 'medium' isn't actually an accurate description of what I do. I regard myself as a worker for spirit, a sensitive worker granted, but a worker nevertheless. It's my job to get on and work on the spirit world's behalf.

I put down the book and thought about it for a second. The meaning was quite clear. It was telling me to get on with my job and to do it as an 'instrument' of spirit.

I looked into Johnson's life psychically and wrote the piece. I believe he was one of the most brilliant musicians

I've ever heard. But I don't believe the legend about his pact with the devil. If he made a pact with anyone, it was the spirit world. Just like the rest of us. He had got the rewards he deserved.

Metal Guru

As I said at the outset of this book, it doesn't matter what kind of sign you receive from the afterlife. Provided you recognise it and acknowledge it, you have made a connection. And you can use that connection to keep close to the spirit world from then onwards. Wherever and whenever you want.

I have come across a few cases in which famous people, living or dead, have acted as signs. For example, there are several people who hold a special significance for me but the one who seems to crop up most often is Marc Bolan, the former leader of the 1970s rock band T Rex.

My connection to him doesn't stem from the fact that I thought he was a great singer and an extremely cool guy. It is to do with the fact that my dad knew him really well and that, ever since I first became a psychic, his name has cropped up frequently, often in the most bizarre and unpredictable situations.

The most common way he shows up for me is through his music, naturally. If I have put out a thought that I would like a sign from spirit and I then hear either of his songs 'Ride a White Swan' or 'Metal Guru', I know this is significant. If it is the former song, for instance, I might combine its relevance with the symbolism of the swan and probably conclude that the sign is to do with faithfulness and loyalty, the qualities that I associate with the bird.

The signs aren't always purely to do with music, however. One weekend, for example, I was sitting in a room filled with my students when one of them produced a book by the late, great medium Doris Stokes. My student was developing his skills as a psychic and a medium, and had been told to bring the book along by his spirit guide. After randomly opening a page in the book, he handed it to me, saying, 'If you know anyone on that page then that is evidence that the spirit world is around you.'

I glanced down and, sure enough, there was a photograph of Marc in his heyday. I took it as a sign from spirit. Not a particularly important one, but a reassuring one – a reminder and a reaffirmation that the spirit realm was connecting with me.

8 | Colours and Smells

Colours play an important part in the language of signs. As with numbers, it is something that works for most of us on an instinctive level. Almost everyone has a favourite or lucky – or maybe even unlucky – colour. As with most things, these colours are very personal and very subjective. The colour red might make one person feel one way, such as angry for example, but it may make someone else feel completely different.

There are some universal guiding principles, with the basic rules of the chakra system acting a good guide. The ancient Sanskrit chakra system places the seven colours of the rainbow at the centre of things, connecting them with energetic vortices that are located at specific points in the body. According to this system, the root chakra at the base of the spine is red, followed by orange in the solar plexus and green in the heart area. But there are specific colours too for individual organs, so for example the heart is a combination of green and pink.

People can be representative of a colour too. As always, the key thing is to make your own connection between a particular colour and the spirit world. Once that connection is made, it will remain unbreakable. From then on, that colour will be a permanent means of seeing and interpreting signs from the spirit realm.

COLOURS

In The Pink

A very good example of the way in which a colour can be linked to a person concerns a young girl named Chloe. She came through to me one night while I was demonstrating on stage at the Theatre Royal in Norwich with Colin Fry a few years ago.

She was a very strong and warm presence from the beginning. But I also sensed that her passing had caused a lot of pain for those she had left behind. As she continued to connect with me I began to see why. Chloe was a vibrant, very feminine eighteen-year-old girl when she was killed in a car accident. The scale of affection that people felt for her was obvious from the images of her funeral that she was placing in my mind.

What was also obvious from these images was the importance of a particular colour: pink.

Pink had clearly been her favourite colour. Chloe was showing me that she was laid to rest in a pink coffin. All the chief mourners and most of the other guests were wearing something pink, if not an item of clothing then a flower or an accessory. The bouquets that had been piled up at her graveside were almost exclusively pink. I don't think I'd ever seen so much intense and bright colour gathered in one place.

The moment I began describing this pink funeral an arm shot up within a group of ladies sitting in the audience. They weren't direct relatives of Chloe, but they were friends of the family.

I told them that Chloe recognised them but that she was telling me that 'someone is missing'. They all nodded at this. One of them told me that Chloe's mother had wanted to be there that night but she hadn't been able to make it. But they also assured me that whatever Chloe's message was, it would be relayed back to the rest of her family in minute detail.

I know that the message was passed on to the rest of her family because, a few weeks later, one of her relatives came to see me for a private reading. Chloe's message was quite a straightforward one. She wanted her family to know she was safe. And she wanted them to know that she was going to be watching over them. It wasn't hard for me to work out what she intended to use as her main means of sending signs: the colour pink was going to be her calling card, I could tell.

Some time afterwards I was hosting a psychic day in my father's pub in the Cambridgeshire countryside. His pub was rather a good spot for such evenings. Almost every time I'd visited it I'd picked up on some kind of spirit presence.

Midway through the evening a couple came up to me. They told me they had travelled all the way down from

Norwich just to be there. They said they wanted to thank me in person for bringing their daughter through to some friends of theirs when I had demonstrated at the Theatre Royal a few weeks earlier.

It didn't require any psychic abilities for me to guess which of the messages related to them. The lady was wearing a bright pink jacket.

'Are you Chloe's parents, by any chance?' I asked.

They both beamed and nodded. 'Yes, I'm Amanda and this is my husband Chris,' the lady said.

Since then we have become friends. I haven't read for them but we've just bonded all the same. What's been fascinating has been to see how Chloe has communicated with them and me. Predictably, it has been primarily through using the colour pink and, because they have established that the colour pink is one of Chloe's tools for revealing herself to them, they now know to view odd sightings of the colour in a fresh light.

Chloe died at a young age. So some of her signs reveal themselves in modern ways. For instance, her mother went on to the social networking site Facebook one day. She'd had a bad day and was missing Chloe terribly so she had put out the thought to the spirit world that it would be nice to get a sign of some kind.

That same day I got a message from Chloe. She told me to look at the first person who had signed on as my friend on Facebook that day. I looked at the page and told Amanda straight away.

A broad grin broke out on her face when she heard the

name. The first person to sign on as my friend that day had been someone called Pinky Hardcastle. Chloe's mum knew immediately it was a sign from her daughter. Now, she no longer necessarily looks for flowers or smells as signs from Chloe. She and her husband also listen out for songs by the singer Pink. The film *The Pink Panther* is also significant.

Of course, as always, every appearance of the colour pink isn't going to be a special sign for them. They have to ask the spirit world for a sign before they can be given it.

Chloe also comes through to me regularly when I am sitting in circle. Again, it doesn't take me very long at all to work out who is trying to make contact. The room suddenly becomes bathed in a deep, pink light.

She will often help me connect with other people who have passed over. She has helped her parents get in touch with other mums and dads who have lost their children in similar, tragic circumstances.

SMELLS

One of the most evocative things we, as humans, experience are smells. A simple whiff of something familiar can trigger all sorts of images and emotions in our minds. Aromas have an amazing ability to conjure up memories of times past.

So it is no surprise that the spirit world taps into our powerful sense of smell in order to send signs of its presence. I have experienced its power many times.

Old Spice And Talcum Powder

It's a sad fact that a large majority of signs are dismissed by those who don't recognise them for what they are. The spirit world expends a great deal of effort and energy to present evidence of its existence. But in most instances the person for whom a sign is intended doesn't see it. Fortunately, the spirit world is persistent. It understands the nature of its task. And it doesn't give up easily – as I have seen myself on many occasions.

One particular example of this always springs to mind. It took place at one of my regular circles. The various circles and classes in which I sit at my centre and else-where are the highlights of my working week. They are constantly interesting and inspiring to me. It's not just my pupils who learn from them. They teach me a lot too.

We receive all sorts of spirit communications within our circle. But one that was sent to us every week for about six weeks in a row one summer was more memorable than most. It was a very distinctive smell – and I will have to be careful when describing it.

It was one of the longer-serving members of the group, Jo, who first detected it. Jo isn't the quietest of individuals. She also tends to say what's on her mind.

Midway through one circle meeting, as the rest of us were deep in thought, attempting to interpret the energy that was clearly in the room, Jo shouted out, 'Oh my God, what is that smell? It's horrible!'

One or two of the others began sniffing the air. As they did so, their faces crumpled up into the sort of expression you'd get if you'd just stepped on something unpleasant on the pavement. Soon the smell was permeating the entire room.

Looking back on it now, I think Jo and the others might have over-reacted slightly. It wasn't actually that bad a smell. There was a faint, perfumed aroma to it. But there was also a very distinctive acidy undertone, which was like the smell of wee.

'I know what this is signifying,' I said after a moment or two. 'This is someone who has passed over in an old people's home.'

Everyone nodded. 'That's what it is,' Jo said. 'It smells exactly like that in my nan's nursing home.'

Having pinned down the smell, however, we still weren't able to connect it to anyone in the room. Jo's nan was still here with us at the time, although she has since passed over. A few other bits of evidence came through: the sender of the message was an elderly lady and she had passed from a heart problem. But it still didn't connect with anyone.

This didn't surprise me entirely. During my years as a medium I've come to the conclusion that smells are often the most easily overlooked signs. People are more fascinated by sights and sounds and feelings than smells for some reason. Yet the irony is that smells are some of the most potent and accurate signs you can get.

My granddad Stan, for instance, always used to smell of Old Spice and the soap that he used to put on his shaving brush. It was a very specific smell. No one else smelled like that. He still uses that smell to let me know he is around today. If I get that familiar whiff in my nostrils I don't have to think about it all. I just say, 'Hello, Granddad, what do you want?'

I was sure that the smell that had appeared in our circle would mean something significant to someone. I was also sure that the spirit world wouldn't rest until the message reached its intended recipient.

Sure enough, when we gathered for our circle again the following week, the same smell came through. The reaction wasn't so bad this time. But the response to the energy that was accompanying the smell was the same. No one recognised it.

The same smell appeared every week for about six weeks. And then we extended the circle to include a couple more members.

One of them was a youngish girl called Melissa. No sooner had we begun the first circle with the new members than the familiar smell came through. It was slightly stronger than it had been in previous weeks and again produced a few strong reactions.

Again we let the energy behind the smell come through. Once more it was an elderly lady. This time, however, she was very specific. She was looking to connect with her granddaughter. She began describing her. As she did so, it became more and more obvious that the girl was sitting in the room.

It was Melissa.

Melissa received a detailed and rather touching message

from her nan who had passed over a year earlier. The old lady had, as we suspected, spent her final days in a nursing home. She made everyone giggle when she told Melissa that she had been happy there although she didn't like the smell. 'The cleaners never cleaned the place properly,' she complained.

We could all vouch for that.

The smell never materialised again. The spirit world had helped Melissa's nan make contact with her. It didn't need to bring the smell through in that environment again.

There were a couple of wonderful things about that sign. For me, it was proof of the persistence of the spirit world, a demonstration of how determined they can be when they want to establish contact with this physical world. What was also so great was the way in which Melissa had been given a really powerful tool which she could now use in her dealings with the spirit world.

Just like I immediately knew how to interpret the smell of my Old Spice and shaving soap, so she would always know what that acidy, talcum powder smell represented. She was new to mediumship and the psychic world. It was going to be a great advantage to have that kind of hotline to spirit.

In the months that followed she used it a lot. Melissa told me that she sniffed the distinctive aroma quite often, not just in her home but elsewhere as well. It was rare that anyone else picked up on it. Once or twice people had begun turning up their noses and looking around for the culprit. But that was about it.

For Melissa it was always a welcome aroma. It was her own, very personal way of keeping in touch with her nan.

Smoke Gets In Your Eyes

One weekend, I went to stay with my mum and dad in their pub in the countryside. I enjoy staying there, not least because it is a fascinating old building that has always surprised me with its psychic resonance.

Since my dad had taken over as landlord I'd been there several times and on almost every occasion something had happened. And so it proved again on this visit.

My mum and dad had mentioned to me that they had picked up on the smell of cigarette smoke in the pub's main bar. Since smoking had been banned from all public houses and restaurants a few years earlier, there was no way it could have been a member of my dad's clientele. He had created a smoking area outside and no one had actually lit up inside the pub for years.

The moment I'd walked into the pub that weekend, I'd smelled it too. It was only when we sat down for a chat late one evening in a particular spot that it began to make sense to me.

My dad was sitting on a stool with his foot up on another stool next to him. As I looked at the second stool I got a powerful feeling about it. 'There is a man who sits here regularly, isn't there?' I said.

'Yes,' my mum said, with a puzzled look on her face. 'Old Fred.'

'And his wife has passed over to spirit a few years ago.'

'Yes,' she said. 'Mabel.'

'Well, you know that powerful cigarette smoke smell you keep spotting in here?' I said.

'Ye-es,' my mum said, looking worried now.

'The cigarette smoke is coming from this lady.'

'What do you mean?' my mum asked.

'She comes to see him and when she comes that's the smell she brings with her.'

'Can't we get rid of it somehow?' my mum wondered.

'Well, the only way that's going to happen is if he acknowledges it as a sign. Then he'll know she's around and she won't need to do it any more,' I explained.

My mum looked at my dad and he looked back at her. They then both looked at me. 'You haven't met old Fred, have you?' they both said.

'If we told him Mabel was coming in here to check on him we'd never see him again,' my dad said. 'I'd rather have the smell of smoke in here than do that,' he added.

Smoke Signals

My friend Alison tells a lovely story about the sign she received one day a few years ago. She had been reading a book by the well-known psychic Betty Shine. In the book Betty asked her readers to place their fingers on a particular spot on a particular page and to send out a thought to the spirit world. If they did so, she promised, they would soon be rewarded by a sign or message.

Alison wasn't entirely convinced by this. She is actually quite a level-headed person and has a healthy scepticism about a lot of things connected to the world of medium-ship and spiritualism. However, out of curiosity, she did as she was told and duly put her finger on the designated spot on the page before putting out a thought. But as she did so she also said: 'Come on then, Betty, show me what you can do.'

She fully expected nothing to happen. But just a few minutes later all the smoke alarms in her house went off. For a minute or two she ran around the house looking to find the fire. But there was nothing. Nor was there any hint of smoke anywhere in the house. She was alone there and no one in the house smoked cigarettes.

The alarms were quite new and were regularly checked. They had never gone off before. And they have never gone off since.

'I don't believe in coincidence,' she told me afterwards.

She remains convinced that it was a sign, or perhaps more accurately a smoke signal, specially sent from the spirit world.

I have no doubt she is right.

Meat and Potato Pie

I've often sensed the presence of the spirit world through picking up on an aroma, perhaps some aftershave or perfume. But I've also seen people connect to someone on the Other Side by identifying more unusual smells.

It happened one weekend while I was sitting in a circle with some friends. The energy levels were very good and we'd brought through some strong messages. The hour or so we were due to spend sitting together was drawing to a close when everyone started sniffing the air and exchanging really quizzical looks.

'What's that smell?' one friend asked.

'It's sort of sweet but meaty as well,' I said.

'It smells like a pie,' another circle member noted.

It was another member of the group, Sue, who pinned down the precise nature of the smell. 'I think it's my gran's meat and potato pie,' she said.

Sue explained that she had been smelling this aroma for quite some time now. 'I get it all day long in the house. Even when I've got the oven off. I can be in the bathroom upstairs sometimes and I get the whiff of her pie,' she said. 'But I've never really accepted it's a sign of her presence.'

I remember smiling at her and saying: 'Wonder no more!' There was absolutely no doubt in my mind. 'If she's carrying it around your house and now she's manifested it in a room full of twenty people, I think it's pretty clearly your gran,' I said to Sue.

I continued, 'What more does she need to do for you? Give her a break – she's been working very hard to get through!'

Sign Language: If At First You Don't Succeed . . .

There are so many ways that you can communicate with a loved one who has passed. Yet so many opportunities are missed. So many people experience something strange or get a feeling of a spirit presence and just head off automatically to see a medium. Mediums like me offer validations of the signs. But we could all be having conversations on a daily basis with spirit on our own. All we have to do is to validate the signs ourselves.

For instance, if you think you have felt a tingling sensation from someone touching you and you think it is a relative, ask them to make themselves known. For example, simply say something along the lines of: 'If that was you, Dad, do it again. If that was you, Nan, do it again.'

If you think a spirit is responsible for a light being switched on and off, perform an experiment. Say to the spirit: 'If that is you, then put that light on.' If it comes on but that's still not enough for you, say: 'Now switch it off.' You can do the same thing with smells, flashing lights, candles, sounds – anything really.

I feel sorry for spirits whose efforts to connect fall on stony ground. They have made an enormous effort, all for nothing. Everyone expects spirits to do all the work. But we need to do some of the heavy lifting as well. One good way to think about it is this: imagine if that person was physically here still and you were having a conversation. If you didn't quite hear what was said the first time or you were distracted when that person showed you something, what would you do? You would ask them to repeat themselves, to do it again. Treat spirits the same way. If at first they don't succeed, let them try and try again. They will reward you for it.

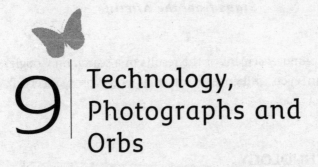

9 | Technology, Photographs and Orbs

It is sometimes difficult to fully comprehend just how omnipresent the spirits of those who have passed over are here in the earthly domain. When I tell people that the spirit world is around us all the time, they often nod their heads as if they get it, but I can tell they don't. Most people don't quite understand how spirit permeates and operates in every corner of our existence. I really don't blame them for this: it is an incredibly hard concept to grasp. It is only in recent years that I have myself begun to appreciate the ways in which the spirit world is able to influence and shape events on the earthly plane.

I've seen it work in all sorts of amazing ways. And I have seen it deliver signs in ways that I wouldn't have believed possible unless I'd witnessed them with my own eyes and ears. I now know that the spirit world is at work in much more subtle and mysterious ways than most people could ever imagine. Sometimes it still even surprises me.

One of the things that has amazed me the most in recent years is the realisation that the spirit world can make use of the new technologies around us. It is capable of changing emails and text messages, altering the images on computer screens or the results of a search on Google. It can even influence events that occur on a Facebook page.

TECHNOLOGY

Changing the Words
One of the most striking examples of how spirits can influence the technological world around us concerns a lady called Angie, who came to me for a reading. I really liked Angie, she was a very warm and sensitive lady. She had suffered a lot of heartache and had a difficult relationship with her family. She was looking for a way forward in her life.

Angie particularly missed her mother, who had passed quite recently. To her delight her mother had come through in the reading and given her a very moving message.

Her mother was not the only spirit to make itself known during that reading, however. To Angie's astonishment, I put her in touch with the baby boy which she had lost during pregnancy. He had some very specific things he wanted to say to her. She was moved to tears to hear me pass them on.

As is so often the case, Angie didn't understand everything that was related to her during the reading. In the days that followed, however, a lot of things slotted into place. Some of the details that her mother passed on didn't mean anything to her at first, which she admitted was not surprising because she and her family weren't close until the end of her mother's life when, typically, their collective pain had drawn them together. Angie's mother had talked about spending time in Margate, which didn't ring any bells at the time. But when Angie subsequently spoke to her sister, she learned that her mother had spent what she'd described as the best holiday ever there, towards the end of her life.

Another detail that began to make sense later on involved rice pudding. During the reading I'd started talking about how I could see tins of rice pudding and that it was giving me the feeling of comfort. It didn't really register with Angie. She told me she wasn't really a fan of rice pudding.

But again after the reading, Angie had walked into her kitchen to find her son there. He was something of a 'stray' and divided his time between living with his mother and with his friends. Like all sons, his first reaction when he'd got home had been to check out the fridge and the food cupboards. It had been in one of the cupboards that he'd found what Angie described to me as a 'dodgy old tin of rice pudding'.

He was standing there eating it out of the tin with a spoon.

'It's my favourite pud, Mum,' he said, surprised at her reaction.

She couldn't even remember buying rice pudding, she admitted.

As I'd seen in the reading, it was clearly a source of comfort – for both of them. For her son it was comfort food; for her it was a comforting reminder of her son's place in her life.

By far the most memorable aspect of the reading, however, related to a song.

During the reading, her baby son had given Angie two important pieces of information. The first was that his name was James. Angie hadn't known this at the time but that was his father's middle name. This really moved her.

The other crucial element of the message was an instruction. Through me, the baby had said that Angie should listen to a particular song when she got home that evening. It was 'Shine' by the group Take That.

Angie was a self-confessed rocker and wasn't really into Take That. She knew the song, but didn't have a copy of the track at home so she'd immediately gone on the internet to look it up. When she'd Googled the relevant terms the usual list of potential websites had scrolled up in front of her. She'd clicked on one which gave the lyrics to the song.

As the words appeared on screen Angie saw the words, 'I know that you can change, Ange.' However, she had a very strong feeling that the name Ange wasn't in the original lyrics. When, a couple of days later, she got hold of a copy of a CD of the song, her suspicion proved correct. There was absolutely no mention of the name Ange.

To Angie it was a huge moment, one which forced her to look hard at herself and to start to think about changing. Her unborn baby had pointed the way ahead. She told me that she was determined to follow its advice.

To me it was a memorable moment in another way. I had never before encountered a situation in which the spirit world delivered a sign in this way. The fact that it could manipulate and influence the internet in that way really amazed me. It was yet more proof of the omnipresence of the spirit world.

Voices in the Dark

The spirit world can also manifest itself aurally; that is, in the form of sounds and voices. Again, the technological age in which we live allows us to capture this in a way we might not have been able to do years ago.

A while ago, at my centre, we captured something which I'm sure was the voice of a person who had passed into spirit.

Yvette, one of the girls who used to work with me at the centre while training as a medium, had kept picking up on the name 'Charlie' in the circles and workshops she attended there. At one point she kept hearing a voice repeatedly saying the name.

'Let's record it and see what we find,' she had said to another colleague.

That night they left a digital recording device running in the room.

When they played it back the next morning, they heard the name Charlie spoken several times. But they also heard more than that.

I had been away from the centre touring and didn't know anything about this. So when they played a recording to me on the first day I returned to the centre, I had no idea what to expect.

As I sat there concentrating on the tape I heard a distinctive, low, gravelly voice of a man say the word 'Charlie' a couple of times. I then listened as he began to whistle. At first I couldn't make out what it was but eventually I recognised it from my childhood. It was the old children's song, 'Pop Goes The Weasel'.

It was clear to me that this was some kind of reference to Pop, as in a father or grandfather figure. From the energy it was giving out, I had the strong feeling that the spirit had passed over very recently.

I discovered that Yvette's boyfriend, Richard, had recently lost his father, who always used to whistle 'Pop Goes The Weasel'.

The tape was sent away to be checked out and eventually became the subject of a story in *Fate & Fortune* magazine.

The spirit world adapts to the changes in our world. So today it uses all the technology that is available to us, from computers and satnavs to emails, telephone and text messages. I am constantly discovering new ways in which the spirits do this.

A Call in the Night

One of the most spine-tingling experiences I've heard about in recent years was related to me by a lady who came to me for a reading. Her name was Stella Holdsworth. She was a very calm and collected lady. She seemed very much in control of her emotions.

During the reading I had been able to put her in contact with her son, who had passed a few years earlier. It was a lovely if perfectly normal message. He told her how much he loved her and missed her, but reassured her that he was in a safe and happy place.

The only unusual thing during the reading was an exchange that happened about halfway through. I was trying to convey the strong feeling I was getting that he had found peace on the Other Side. But I also felt that part of that peace was down to the knowledge that his mother knew this. I assumed at first that this was because she'd seen other mediums in the past. They must have brought through messages before.

But then he sent me a very particular message. 'It's like I said on the night I passed – I'm fine,' he said through me. I didn't know what this meant, but assumed his mother would. 'Do you understand that?' I asked her.

She looked at me almost surprised that I'd even asked. 'Oh yes, of course,' she said with a quick smile. 'I understand that perfectly well.'

It was an intriguing statement and I asked her about it after the reading was over. 'When he mentioned that he had told you he was fine on the night he passed, what did he mean?'

'Oh, it's quite a long story,' she said, slipping on her coat. 'I'm sure you've heard many like it over the years.'

Even if I had – and I hadn't – I would have been interested. As luck would have it she was my last appointment of the day. So I suggested that we went downstairs for a cup of tea and she could tell me all about it. She was happy to do so.

As we sat down and sipped our teas, she described to me what must have been the most horrendous night any parent could imagine going through.

Her son, Michael, was in his teens and was a good lad, but similar to most teenagers, he was at a stage in life where he wanted to go out and party a lot. Like all mothers, Stella would sit up late waiting for him to come home and, if it got really late, lie in bed waiting for the telltale sound of the front door being opened.

On this particular night, she had waited and waited and waited, but had eventually dropped off to sleep. It had been almost exactly 3 a.m. when she was woken by the ringing of her telephone. It was Michael.

She recognised his voice immediately and at first began chastising him for being out so late. 'Do you realise what time it is?' she grumbled.

'Don't worry, Mum, I'm fine,' Michael replied. His voice sounded quite distorted and distant, so she assumed he was on a mobile in an area with poor reception.

'Where are you, Michael? And what's going on?' she said, quite snappily.

He just repeated what he had said before: 'Don't worry, Mum, I'm fine.'

Stella was about to really lose her temper with him, but before she could say anything more the telephone line went dead.

It took her a while to get back to sleep. She was quite

agitated, she told me. Eventually, however, she nodded off again, but almost immediately the phone rang again.

Bleary-eyed and squinting to see in the dim light, she looked at her clock. It was now 4 a.m. She'd been asleep for less than an hour.

As she answered the phone she expected to hear Michael's voice once more. Instead she heard a voice she didn't recognise.

'Hello, this is the A and E department at St Mary's Hospital. Am I speaking to Mrs Holdsworth?' the lady said.

'Yes,' Stella replied, her pulse rate rising immediately.

'I'm afraid we have your son, Michael, in intensive care here. He has been in an accident. We think you should come here as soon as possible,' the woman said.

Stella told me how she had thrown on a jumper and a pair of jeans, and run downstairs and into her car. The roads were absolutely empty and she got to the hospital in little more than ten minutes.

She knew the hospital well, having been to it many times before to visit a friend who had passed there a year earlier. She ran straight down the main corridor to where she knew the intensive care ward was tucked away at the far end of the building.

She arrived there breathless. 'I'm here to see my son, Michael Holdsworth,' she said.

The lady looked up and then looked down again very quickly, not making eye contact. She then picked up the phone and dialled a number which was picked up almost instantly.

'I have Mrs Holdsworth here in reception,' she said. After a pause she simply said, 'OK,' then again looked up at Stella.

'Mrs Holdsworth, would you mind taking a chair?' she said, pointing at a small seating area. 'The consultant will be over to see you in a minute.'

Stella had a bad feeling immediately she said this and was shaking by the time the consultant arrived. As she'd feared it was bad news, the worst news possible. All she heard were the first three words: 'I'm terribly sorry . . .'

In the days that followed Stella learned a little more about what had happened. Michael had gone with some friends to a local pub for a quiz night. They had then gone back to a friend's house where they had stayed until 2 a.m. Michael and a couple of his friends had then begun walking home down the deserted streets.

All of a sudden a speeding car had come careering towards them, completely out of control. It had ploughed through them and into a wall.

Amazingly the driver escaped unhurt, as did Michael's friends. Michael, however, had borne the brunt of the collision. He had been rushed into an operating theatre where the surgeons had spent an hour vainly trying to save his life.

The one thing that no one had explained, however, was when and where Michael had made the telephone call to his mother. Stella had been too upset to talk to anyone apart from close relatives. A relative of hers spoke to the boys who were with Michael, but neither of them could recall him making a call. As it happened only one of them had a mobile on them, but it had no credit on it.

This left Stella feeling even more confused.

It was when she was given a post mortem report that Stella noticed what time Michael had died. He had been taken into surgery at 2.30 a.m. but had been pronounced dead at just after 3 a.m.

At first Stella thought she must be going mad. He had telephoned her just before 3 a.m. But, according to the records at least, he would have been in the operating theatre at that point. In fact, that was when he must have been fading from life.

'It took me a long time to understand it,' she told me, as we sat together, our tea now turned cold in our cups. 'It was when I went to see a medium that Michael came through and explained it. He told me that he'd been passing over at that precise moment. Somehow he'd been able to get a message through.'

Stella told me that during that reading he'd repeated the same phrase he'd used on the night of his passing and again with me today: 'Don't worry, Mum, I'm fine.'

Stella had been to several demonstrations and seen other mediums in the time since Michael's passing. Each time he'd come through he'd said the same thing.

I knew that spirits have the capacity to make contact very quickly after passing over. Usually it is when the passing was very peaceful. This was one of the earliest messages I'd heard of. It wasn't a unique story, however.

'I did hear of a lady who heard something similar,' I said to Stella.

I then related the story of a woman who lived near me when I was living in north London. She had gone through a remarkably similar experience to the one Stella had endured. Her son had been a passenger in a car when it had skidded off a motorway and crashed. She too had arrived at the hospital, although in her case her son was still in the operating theatre when she got there.

She had been told to wait nearby and had been pacing the corridor nervously waiting for news when she heard what she was certain was her son's voice. He was shouting out the words: 'Mum, Mum.'

Hearing his voice had raised her spirits and her hopes briefly, but within a couple of minutes a nurse had emerged to give her the worst piece of news she'd ever received in her life. Her son had passed over ten minutes earlier.

'But I heard him shouting out just a minute ago,' she had said, confused and distraught. The nurse had given her a sympathetic look and led her away somewhere peaceful before taking her to see her son's body.

Stella sat there nodding as I told the story. Afterwards she produced a tissue from her handbag and dabbed at her eyes.

A New York State of Mind

The signs and messages I receive from the spirit world via music don't always come directly to me. It took a very gifted psychic friend of mine, Paul, to show me that they can be delivered second-hand as well. And they can be delivered via the technologies which now play such an important role in our modern lives.

At first I wasn't sure I believed Paul when he told me that he could channel messages and signs from the spirit world via an iPod or MP3 player. I was even more doubtful when he told me that he could do so simply by stopping a music player randomly and using either the song title or lyrics.

One of the acid tests I use to judge whether something is working psychically is whether my Pops appears. I know he is one of my closest companions on the spirit side. If he shows himself then I believe in what I am being shown.

Paul did a reading for me and threw up three songs. I was there with him so I know he couldn't have manipulated or influenced the iPod he used. He had it on shuffle and was choosing from a song catalogue of thousands. The first song that came up was by the 1980s band Level 42. It was 'Tracy', the very same song that had persuaded Paul himself to listen to my advice on that other occasion that I've mentioned earlier.

I nodded and smiled, but I wondered whether it was beginner's luck. So Paul did it again. In fact, he did it three times.

Each time he came up with songs with a New York connection in them. Two of them had New York in the title. The other was an old love song 'Chanson d'Amour' by Manhattan Transfer.

'Do you understand that?' he asked me.

I simply nodded. As it happened, I'd had a conversation that week with a new agent who was based in London but came originally from New York. She was a New York City girl in every sense of the word.

Paul said he needed to come up with one more song to complete the reading. I had already drawn the message from it. I knew it was telling me that I was meant to somehow work with the agent from New York. How that was going to happen given various complications that were going on in my career at that time, I wasn't sure. But I was sure it was going to happen at some point.

My only concern about the reading was that I hadn't yet had anything from it that was to do with my granddad. And this bothered me. Paul hit the shuffle button once more and up came a song and a band that I had never heard of in my life.

It was 'A Streetcar Named Desire' by a band called Bad Seed. 'What does that mean?' I asked him.

Paul shrugged. 'I can't tell you that, but I can tell you that it means something.'

At home later on that evening I was watching TV and was flicking through the menu, looking for a movie to watch. I love old 1950s movies so was looking at the channels that tended to show these. Suddenly I stopped flicking.

One of the channels was showing *A Streetcar Named Desire* starring Marlon Brando. 'Of course,' I said to myself. I knew that phrase had rung a bell. The song was inspired by the famous film which in turn had been inspired by a famous play.

As I looked at the details I saw that it also starred the great British actress Vivien Leigh. This chimed with a female spirit who had been trying to get some kind of message through to me for the past few days. I sensed I was on to something.

It was when I flicked on the cast of characters that I got my answer. Again, it was something that was tucked away at the back of my mind but I'd forgotten.

Marlon Brando's character in the film was called Stanley, Stanley Kowalski. Even though the character in the film is very challenging, the name Stanley – my grand-dad's name – is always a good omen for me. That was the sign in Paul's iPod reading. From then on I put my reservations to one side and believed in Paul's method. In fact, I even started using it myself.

PHOTOGRAPHS AND ORBS

The spirits of those who have passed over can reveal themselves in a myriad different ways. Sometimes the spirit of the person comes back in their physical form. I have seen this many times during my life, both in séance situations and on other occasions. This was how Pops and my aunt Maisie revealed themselves to me. When a person reveals themselves like this, it is as if they are sitting there in the room with you. This is not something that is going to happen to very many people, however. Such signs of the afterlife are rare.

More commonly, only their faces or other parts of their body are visible. I once did a reading for a lady in which all I could see was a very distinctive-looking arm, covered in tattoos with gold rings on his hand.

Sometimes these images are projected on to walls or ceilings. Sometimes they appear on the pages of books. But by far the most common form of spirit appearance that I encounter nowadays is in photographs, where the images of those who have passed over appear in the form of orbs.

Orbs are a phenomenon that is little known outside the psychic community. But they are real and they are a powerful sign of life on the Other Side.

What is an orb? Well, essentially it is a spirit light. It is the first formation in which a spirit is able to manifest itself. It usually appears in the form of a glistening sphere, almost like a drop of water captured falling through the air. Within that sphere, often, the very essence of the person who has passed over is visible in spirit form.

It has only been in the last few years that I have come to understand orbs. It began when a man took some photographs during a circle at my centre. I'd given him permission to do this, I hasten to add. It wouldn't have been something I'd have approved of in normal circumstances. However, the guy had explained to me that he had read up about orbs online and he had learned it was possible to see the faces of spirits within them. They most commonly manifested themselves during psychic or mediumistic activity. I was intrigued to see what his camera picked up.

The guy had used a very powerful digital camera. Sure enough, hovering in the air, somewhere above my head, was a small, very bright ball of light. It looked like a pearl from a necklace was being dropped from the ceiling.

Thanks to the power of digital photography, we were able to enlarge it on a computer. At first it was hard to make out the shapes contained within it. But then a thought occurred to me. Why are we assuming a spirit would inhabit our dimension in the same way as we inhabit it? In other words, it might be inside out or upside down for all we knew.

I asked the guy to flip the image round 180 degrees so that it was upside down. It took a second or two for the computer to perform the flip, but the moment the up-turned image appeared on the screen I recognised what it was showing me.

'It's Paddy,' I said.

As I've mentioned, Paddy was one of my original spirit guides, a potato farmer from Ireland. He had remained a constant presence in my psychic life. I'd seen his face often while we were connected.

It was an amazing moment. But it was far from the last. Since then I have discovered many stories of spirits that have signalled their presence in the form of orbs.

A Wall of Faces

When a friend of mine, Mary, returned from the Polish city of Krakow, she did so with a huge collection of photographs. Amongst the usual 'touristy' snaps of Mary and her partner standing alongside statues and outside churches, there were some more sombre images.

Mary had spent part of her break visiting some of the German concentration camps that had been built in the area. The infamous Auschwitz and Birkenau camps as well as the smaller Krakow-Plaszow were all within easy range of her hotel in Krakow.

Mary had found the camps every bit as powerful and emotionally overwhelming as she'd expected them to be. We've all seen films like *Schindler's List* and watched those heartbreaking black and white documentaries about what the Nazis did to millions of Jews. But coming face to face with the reality of it was a deeply unsettling experience, Mary told me.

Walking around the grim accommodation blocks was hard enough. But, unsurprisingly, it was the gas chambers themselves that were the most distressing. Mary has a strong psychic gift and she told me she felt a very dark and powerful spirit presence in there.

As we pored over some of Mary's images from the camps, I noticed a few odd shapes in the background. In particular, up against a white wall inside one of the gas chambers I saw a collection of circles. When we enlarged the images on her camera's LCD screen we saw a group of orbs, very similar to the ones that had appeared in my photographs.

We downloaded them onto a computer and began looking at them more closely. As we did so we both began to see the unmistakeable forms of human faces. They weren't shouting out or screaming. They were simply staring out, almost helplessly.

It reminded me of the faces of the survivors that the British and American troops found when they liberated the camps. It was as if they were in a dream-like state, not part of this world. In a way, of course, they weren't part of this world even when they were in the physical world. Those camps were the nearest thing there has been to hell on earth.

Seeing the faces sent an unbelievably strong shiver running down our spines. Mary is a very open-minded person, however, and didn't want to jump to too many conclusions.

Also, I had told her about something I'd read about digital cameras naturally producing little light objects in some conditions. Not every light you see on a digital picture is going to be the spirit of a person who has passed over. Far from it. Orbs are relatively rare things.

Mary wanted to be sure that we really had seen what we thought we'd seen. So she took the images and showed them to other people, most of whom were not connected to the centre and were not psychic in any way.

She didn't give any explanation about where she'd taken the photos. They didn't know that the faceless white walls in the background were the inside of a Nazi gas chamber.

They almost all said the same thing when Mary showed them the enlargements of the orbs. They said they could see people inside them. One person even said he thought they looked like Jewish people, crammed inside a concentration camp.

That was enough for Mary. She was now certain that she'd been given a sign by the spirit world.

It was clear to me too that there must have been an incredibly highly-charged spiritual energy in that concentration camp. Mary had captured it on film. She had seen the spirits of hundreds of Nazi victims.

It was a consolation to know that, having left the horrors of the gas chambers, they had reached the peace and tranquillity of the spirit world. But the images haunted us both for a long time afterwards.

Sign Language: How to Use Signs in Your Life

When people hear about how I use signs in my life, they often ask how they can do the same. I usually tell them the same thing. It's easy to see signs all around us. But the hard part is knowing which ones are being delivered to us by the spirit world. To be able to do this, we need to know what to look for and when to look for it.

In general terms, most signs will come when we ask to be shown them. It is when the spirit world has a warning to deliver or needs somehow to intervene to make you do something or stop you from doing something, that they can appear out of the blue. So let's consider some practical examples which might help you understand how to deal with the former.

A Career Move

Let's suppose that you are facing a dilemma about your job. Perhaps you are happy enough in the job you have, but you have been asked to go for an interview for another position which perhaps offers more money and more responsibility. What signs should you look out for as you make up your mind?

If you ask the spirit world for help and you are not meant to take the job, the first thing they will do is put obstacles in your way. So, for instance, if you are heading for the interview, everything will slow down. The buses, the trains and the underground will suffer delays. If you're driving the traffic lights will be against you. If this happens to you it should set your mind thinking: is this the right move for me?

However, spirit communication has to be a two-way thing. You have to make your own decisions. What will happen is that your own consciousness will start pondering on the matter.

If you are meant to do the job, then you will see signs around you relating to the company or the employer. For example, let's say you were going for a job with a company called Morgan. If it was the right thing to take the job, you would start seeing the name in an out of context way. You wouldn't be looking for it but it would nevertheless manage to catch your eye. You might see a movie poster with Morgan Freeman, the American actor, on it. You might see a Morgan sports car. You might see someone on a train reading a book by Piers Morgan.

Those things would begin to add up and create a very positive attitude towards the job.

You can build on this by looking for other positives or

negatives that relate to signs you know apply to you. So if you know your own lucky numbers, see if they relate to the company. Perhaps their HQ is at an address that matches your best numbers.

Look for signs in the names of other members of staff. If you have a strong positive – or negative – association with a particular name, see if the list of directors or other staff contains this name.

If I saw that there were a lot of people with the name Stanley in their first or surnames I would feel reassured and safe about the company. If I saw something connected to the company that related to the firm Morgan Stanley I would be very reassured because Stanley is the name that I really trust. That, combined with Morgan, would constitute a really positive sign, for me.

A Marriage Proposal

I know several people who have been terribly torn by a proposal of marriage. In some cases, they have looked out for signs.

The first thing I would do is look at the 'background noise'. A good way to look at that would be if you are constantly hearing references to marriages, proposals, adverts for engagement rings.

If, on the other hand, the background buzz you are hearing is to do with broken relationships or divorces, then you should take that on board.

If the songs on the radio were all to do with soul mates, natural attraction and enduring love then that would be a positive sign. So songs like '(Everything I Do) I Do It For You' by Bryan Adams or 'Evergreen' by Will Young, which might indicate that you could be right for each other.

But if the songs were all about break-ups, perhaps classics like 'I Will Survive' by Gloria Gaynor or 'Goodbye to Love' by The Carpenters, then this may well be the spirit world trying to get a message to you.

You should also keep an eye out for significant symbols relating to love and romance. And, if you saw an animal or animal symbol in an unusual or unexpected context, that might also be a good sign. So if, for instance, you saw a swan, which I believe usually represents commitment and fidelity, that would be very encouraging. If something unusual happened to you relating to a dog, that would be good too. Dogs often symbolise loyalty.

On a deeper level, if a crow was to appear in an odd way, it might be a sign that you need to stop and take a good look inside yourself. The crow is a sign of introspection, so it might be saying 'don't make a snap decision, don't rush it, think about what you really want'.

Colours would be another important indicator. Pink or green are good heart colours so if you were to see them in an odd context, that too would be a good sign.

You should also look at the symbolism of marriage. If, for instance, you saw a diamond, in an out-of-context way, that would also be a good sign. So, for instance, if you heard the song 'Diamonds Are A Girl's Best Friend' in an unusual context, or you were stuck in traffic behind a van with a sign that had the word diamond in it, that would be a good, positive sign.

10 | Music and Sounds

I suppose if there is one thing that makes me different from most other mediums, it is the way that I use music a lot to convey messages from the spirit world. It's something that I developed early on during my career.

Ever since I was a young girl, music has played a huge part in my life. It wasn't so much that I was musical myself; it was more that I always felt music had a huge ability to change my mood and consequently to change the way I felt and saw the world. It also provided an escape. During bad times, I would retreat into my bedroom and listen to the radio or my cassette player. I would let the music wash over me and suddenly my troubles didn't seem so immense. I've turned to music to escape from my worries on more occasions than I'd like to admit.

As soon I began to understand how the spirit world influences our lives in the physical world, I began to see that music had an even greater significance, however. It is one of the tools that the spirits can use to guide, advise and protect us.

It was while I was training as a medium, attending the famous Arthur Findlay College near Stansted, that I first began to see that music played a role. Particular pieces of music would come on in my car radio, often echoing events that had happened or were about to happen. I soon realised they weren't being played by accident. I began to notice that particular pieces of music would crop up at important times in my life. Invariably these songs would have a title or include lyrics that contained something that related very specifically to what was troubling me. I began to see that it was the spirit world communicating with me. Today, I consider music to be one of the most potent and universal signs from the afterlife. I am constantly coming across examples of its power.

The spirit world works with what's going on in your own mind. Whatever is in your memory bank, they will use. If you are a football fan they will tap into that, for instance. Given that I am the sort of person who would always rather be listening to music than to a television in the background, I do have a lot of songs in my own memory banks. Which means, when I am looking for connections with spirit, I tend to pick up on a lot of songs.

If, for instance, I were to connect with a lady called Jean, I might hear lyrics such as 'Cheer up, sleepy Jean' from the Monkees' song 'Daydream Believer', or hear 'Billie Jean' by Michael Jackson. If I were to connect with someone who is – like me – a fan of Tottenham Hotspur, I might hear the old fan favourite song 'Nice One, Cyril'.

The sign doesn't necessarily have to come from music heard on the radio. It can come in all sorts of forms, such as a mention in a conversation on talk radio.

When my friend the numerologist Didier Boyer died, I was driving around and thinking: 'I really need to know that he is OK; I need a sign that he has safely passed over.'

That particular day, I was being given a lift by a male friend, Jeremy, and rather than Heart or Capital FM he had talkSPORT blaring away on his car radio. No sooner had I asked for some evidence about Didier than his name came up. They were talking about the Chelsea footballer Didier Drogba, but not just in passing. They were repeating his name again and again, each time using his first name and surname. It was Didier Drogba this and Didier Drogba that. (It always amazes me that these guys can find so much to say about a bloke whose job it is to kick a ball into a large net!) It immediately made me feel a connection.

Didier Drogba is a connection that I now look out for. When it appears in answer to a request from me, I know Didier's presence is near.

The Dragonfly and the Bumblebee

Early on I developed a very particular way of using music. For some reason which I've never fully understood I would always instinctively listen for the third song that came on the radio and draw something from that. In numerology, the number three is often associated with fresh starts and new beginnings, so that may have something to do with it.

My method has worked out pretty well for me. Music has provided me with hugely important signs about my relationships, my career and the direction I was taking in life in general. It has even helped me in my travels.

A few years ago, shortly after I broke through as a medium and appeared on the television show *Psychic Private Eyes*, I was asked to go to Los Angeles with my fellow medium Colin Fry and our mutual agent. We were planning to meet various people about possible new shows and even talking about organising a tour to the US at some point.

In theory I should have been over the moon to get such an invitation. I'd always wanted to visit America. But, instinctively, I wasn't sure if travelling to the US was going to be right for me at that point in my life. Yes, it was going to be exciting, of course. But was it what I really should be doing right then?

So, in my mind, I started sending out a request to the spirit world that I needed a sign. I wanted it to show me that I was going to the right place at the right time. I wanted to know that this planned trip to America was what I should be doing. Above all, I wanted to know that this was what spirit wanted for me.

Over the course of the next few days I listened to the radio a lot and made a point of checking the third songs. It was uncanny. I kept getting the song 'California Dreamin'' by The Mamas & the Papas and 'Coming to America' by Neil Diamond.

And that wasn't the only thing that happened. Everywhere I went, people seemed to be talking about something relating to America, whether it was President

Bush or a new TV series or American food. That was all I could hear in my head. Eventually I got the message. The spirit world was telling me to go.

Colin Fry and I get on wonderfully well. We really complement each other, both as mediums and as people, partly because we are very different. I have for a long time associated myself with a dragonfly and, as I have told Colin himself, I see him as a bumblebee, full of nervous energy and activity as he tunes in to the vibrations of the spirit world. We often joked about it. We called ourselves the Dragonfly and the Bumblebee. In fact, when we are building our energy up before we go on stage together for a performance, I often hear that classical music piece 'Flight of the Bumblebee' in my head.

Finally arriving in LA was – for me anyway – a special moment in my life. We were picked up at the airport by a limousine and whisked off to the trendy Melrose district of the city. As we drove along the freeway, I looked up into the Hollywood Hills, saw the famous old sign and smiled. Arriving in Melrose, I was even more excited. We were surrounded by beautiful people and cool shops. It was everything I'd dreamed of – and maybe more.

We were booked into this beautiful boutique hotel. I was tired after the long flight and, as a bellboy escorted me up in the lift to my room, I was looking forward to a shower to wake me up a little. We had a meeting scheduled later that evening.

As it turned out I didn't need a shower to shake me out of my slump in energy. The bellboy led me into a lovely, tastefully decorated room. But as I scanned the walls I couldn't believe my eyes. There were two or three tasteful paintings dotted around the room, including a very large and colourful one right above the bed. It showed a dragonfly and a bumblebee.

I was so bowled over by seeing that painting above my bed that I took a photograph of it with my mobile phone. When I went downstairs and showed it to Colin, he just burst into a huge smile.

How on earth could that be anything other than a sign? How could this mean anything other than 'welcome to LA – you're meant to be here'? And so it proved.

I had a great time, and met some really interesting people, including a lady connected to Oprah Winfrey. The connections I made there are still playing a part in my life and may well do so again in the future.

I have that photograph of the dragonfly and the bumblebee still.

'Je Ne Regrette Rien'

On the morning of 18 March 2009, I was in my studio waiting for a phone call. A lady somewhere up in Scotland had booked a telephone reading with me but had been delayed for some reason or another. I used the extra time it gave me to catch up on some paperwork.

I had a huge backlog of things to deal with, but I didn't get very far with it, unfortunately. Sitting at my desk, I suddenly felt a very strong energy, a male energy. I couldn't see the man who was transmitting it, but I could feel a quality to the energy that I'd come across before. It was displaced and heavy. It was the energy of someone who had committed suicide.

People often ask me how I can feel things like this and I find it very hard to answer. So much of my work is instinctive, based on intuition and feeling. It is difficult to put it into words. The only analogy I can provide is that a natural death feels to me like going down a fairground slide. It is a smooth, free-flowing process. There is nothing holding you back. A suicide, on the other hand, feels very different. I sense that I am travelling down a slide still, but in this case it feels a lot heavier, a lot slower and more restricted. It is as if I am not really meant to be going down.

Initially, I thought the energy was that of a man who knew someone who was taking part in a class at the centre that morning. I knew that the guy taking part in the class had a friend who had taken his own life six months or so earlier, and who had come through before.

I was ready to tell the man in spirit that I knew who he was, when I got a tiny flash of physical detail that stopped me. I saw his hair and realised that he had a full head of jet-black curls. The guy who had committed suicide months earlier had had a shaven head. He also seemed a lot older than this person.

I was thrown by this. I didn't know who it was, even though I felt I should. The energy wasn't fading so I focussed a little harder. Suddenly all I could hear in my mind was the legendary French singer Edith Piaf, singing her most famous song, 'Non, Je Ne Regrette Rien' ('No, I Regret Nothing').

I was interrupted by the sound of the phone ringing. It was the lady from Scotland calling for her phone reading. As I began I wondered whether this man was trying to communicate with her. I had to be careful about the way I framed my reading. I didn't want to upset her if this person had nothing to do with her. And it turned out that he didn't.

Instead, I brought through her father, a very light and seemingly happy spirit. There was certainly nothing about him that suggested suicide. Indeed, I identified the fact that he'd died of a stroke.

In an attempt to try to work out what was happening, I asked the lady whether either Edith Piaf or the song 'Non, Je Ne Regrette Rien' meant anything to her. They didn't. I wondered perhaps whether her father had been a man who had no regrets in life. 'Oh, I'm sure he had a lot,' she said.

I realised that this didn't really fit. The suicide message was not for this lady. It had been sent by someone unconnected to her.

With the reading over I finished my paperwork, joined in another class and then headed home. I got into the house at around 5.30 p.m. and checked my answer machine and my emails.

My eyes immediately jumped to an email that had been sent around lunchtime. It was simply headed: 'Didier Boyer'.

It was from a mutual friend of ours and was very brief.

It said that Didier had committed suicide in the early hours of the morning. He had been found by a friend who had tried to revive him, but it was all too late. It seemed like he had planned the whole thing meticulously.

For a moment or two I sat there, stunned. But then I began to cry. Didier was one of the most vibrant, clever and warm-hearted people I'd ever met. He had shown absolutely no sign of being unhappy or worried about anything in his life. In fact, his life was going really well. He had plans to do more television and to write a book. People were starting to take his work seriously and he was being invited to read all over Europe. It didn't make sense, but then suicides often don't – especially for those left behind, I thought to myself.

It was then that I started hearing the familiar strains of the song I'd heard earlier in the day: Edith Piaf singing 'Non, Je Ne Regrette Rien'. As soon as I heard it I knew that Didier was OK. Even though I found his death hard to understand, I knew that he had left this life harbouring no great unfulfilled dreams or hopes.

In the days that followed, I learned a bit more about what had happened. I guessed that there was going to be a significance to the timing of his death. Knowing Didier, the numbers would have had to have been aligned correctly. It turned out that he had taken his own life at a particular time that had a special numerological significance to him. So too did the date.

I sense him around me still and connect him with several signs, most obviously some of the numbers that I know were important to him. His name too resonates often for me. But it is that song which will be my most powerful connection to Didier.

Although I still miss him terribly, as do all his friends and family, there is some comfort in the thought that he regretted nothing in this life. And I'm sure he won't regret anything in the next one either . . .

A Passing Motorbike

One of the most obvious signs of someone's presence I've received in recent years came one afternoon when I was doing a reading for a lady at my centre in Waltham Abbey.

She had lost her son tragically a year or so earlier. I was able to connect with him and felt his presence very strongly in the room. I could even smell his aftershave.

His mother was really emotional about talking to him, but he didn't seem to have much to say. In fact, all he could keep saying to me was, 'Listen, listen.'

At first I wasn't quite sure what he meant by this. When I asked his mother she didn't seem to understand it either. But then, as we both sat in the room in silence, we began to hear something.

The centre is set on a pedestrianised street. Cars and other vehicles are not allowed to drive down it. So the only sound you normally hear outside is that of people passing by.

Today, however, there was the unmistakeable sound of a motorbike. It was doubly odd because it wasn't as if the bike was simply driving by. It kept fading slightly then returning. The rider was clearly driving up and down the street for some reason. It was almost as if it was passing by our front window in an effort to be noticed.

Eventually I got up and looked out. It was a guy in full riding gear – leathers and a helmet. He was riding a Honda CBR bike.

When I returned the mother was in floods of tears. 'That's what he wanted me to listen out for,' she said. 'That was his bike. He drove a bike like that. He even wore leathers just like that.'

It turned out her son had lived and breathed motorbikes. He wasn't a wild kid in any sense. In fact he belonged to a motorcycling club and took part in organised races.

He had died in a terrible road accident on his bike. It hadn't been his fault, apparently. He had been hit by another vehicle when its driver had lost control. He had been killed instantly.

It was odd because I heard another similar story not long afterwards.

A friend called Lee had asked for a sign that his brother was still around. He had passed eight years earlier, aged just twenty-one. His brother missed him terribly and thought about him all the time.

Within minutes of putting out this thought he had heard the song 'Angels' by Robbie Williams on the radio. It had been the music at his brother's funeral. It was also a song that his brother liked to sing when he regularly did karaoke.

More significantly, however, Lee had also heard the

sound of motorbikes passing by outside his house. Again, it wasn't a common sound in his neck of the woods. It was usually a quiet road. His brother, too, had been a really keen motorbike rider. Lee was convinced the two sounds had been a sign from his brother. And I'm sure he was right.

From the Mouths of Babes

At times the spirit world manifests itself through the mouths of others. Words that you would never have expected to hear can be spoken by the least likely person in order to deliver a powerful piece of evidence that the spirit world is present.

The most extraordinary example of such a sign I ever encountered came one Saturday morning, when I was doing readings at a psychic shop and centre called The White Witch early on during my career.

Until then it had been a fairly uneventful morning. I had read for a series of people, delivering a range of messages from loved ones and friends on the Other Side. I'd just had my morning cup of coffee, when a rather flustered-looking young lady arrived for her reading, pushing a buggy with a baby inside it.

'I'm really sorry,' she said, slightly breathless. 'I was meant to have had a babysitter this morning but I was let down at the last minute. Is there any way I can bring my little girl into the sitting with me? She'll be as good as gold, I promise.'

It really doesn't bother me if people bring their children into readings. Provided they behave themselves and don't make too much noise, obviously. So when we went through to the reading room, the baby came with us. And, as she'd promised, the baby was perfectly behaved.

The lady's mother came through to me during the reading, but, for some reason, I found it hard to pass on any evidence of her presence. In my head she was talking away about how pleased she was to see her granddaughter in the room. 'Isn't she lovely, looks just like her grand-dad,' she said at one point.

Before I can pass on a worthwhile message to a client, I need to give them solid, tangible evidence that their loved one is present in spirit form. Until I have done this I can't really deliver a message. The recipient must recognise the spirit.

The fact that all this lady wanted to talk about was a grandchild whose presence was plain for all to see was of no use to me. It left me floundering and a little frustrated.

After a while I began apologising to the lady for not getting anything worthwhile from her mother. 'I can see her and she's clearly your mother, but she's not showing me anything that I can use because she's so pleased to see the baby,' I said.

It was at this point that something completely unexpected happened. All of a sudden, and for no apparent reason, the baby became quite excitable. She wasn't upset or anything like that. She just seemed to come alive. She then spoke a single word: 'Nan.'

The lady and I both looked at each other, open-mouthed.

'What did she just say?' her mother said, looking at me.

'She said "Nan",' I said, still shaking my head in disbelief. Then I asked, 'Has she spoken before?'

'No. Never. She's only four months old.'

This was a few years ago, during the days when psychics were permitted to make tape recordings of their readings. When we played back the tape it was as clear as day. The baby had said 'Nan'.

We also heard a woman's voice saying the name 'Frances'.

This was a clear sign of her presence. In many ways it was more direct and persuasive than any message that I'd been able to give her daughter.

It was a moment that has stuck in my memory ever since because it resonated on so many levels. On one level it reminded me of that old expression about the truth coming 'out of the mouths of babes'. How true had that been in this instance? And on a deeper level it opened my eyes to a truth that I've begun to appreciate more and more over the years.

It taught me to always expect the unexpected where the spirit world is concerned.

Dance With My Father Again

It was a Sunday morning shortly before Christmas and I was driving to the centre for a mid-morning class. As always, I had the radio on. I was listening to Heart FM if memory serves me correctly. The mood of the music had been fairly lively when I'd set off, but it soon turned more sombre and emotional.

The first song that came on was Robbie Williams singing 'Angels'. I have lost count of the number of people who have told me that they had this song played at a loved one's funeral. It seems to touch a chord that few other modern songs have done. By the time it was coming to an end I found myself singing along quietly to the oh-so familiar chorus.

The next song that came on was an all-time favourite of mine, 'Dance With My Father Again' by the late, great American soul singer Luther Vandross. This, again, is a song that I have heard before in a spiritual context. Naturally, it's usually in connection with people who are missing or mourning a father who has passed over to the Other Side.

I have always been a bit of a softie when it comes to love songs and very emotive lyrics. But even I was surprised when I found myself welling up during the song. By the end I was reaching for a handkerchief in my handbag.

I was thinking that I'd like to hear a more upbeat song next, something that would lift my soul a little. But the very gentle chords that began filling the car were just the opposite.

I knew the song immediately. It was Michael Bublé singing his huge hit, 'Home'. It was at this point that I began to wonder whether something was going on here.

This too was a very resonant song for me. I think it is a piece of music that has a deep spiritual meaning. To me, it doesn't only refer to reaching our earthly home. It is also about going home in a spiritual sense, passing over into the spirit world. I had heard it playing in my head before during readings. Often, it was connected to loved ones who had passed over very recently.

By now I was approaching Waltham Abbey and was minutes from the Dragonfly Centre. As I drove through the streets, for some reason, another member of our class, a lady called Mary, suddenly appeared in my thoughts. She was due to be at the centre this morning. I had a feeling this music had some significance to her.

As I approached the car park near my centre, the Michael Bublé song was coming to its climax. I had tears in my eyes. As I parked my car, I noticed another class member, Anna, climbing out of her car.

Weirdly, I could see that she was crying. She was dabbing away at her face with a handkerchief. I didn't feel like I should say anything, but I didn't need to. Anna was soon explaining what had happened.

'That was odd,' she said as she walked towards me and headed towards the centre.

'What was?' I said.

'Well, I've just been listening to Heart FM on the radio and they've just played three songs that made me cry,' she said.

I just nodded.

'Yeah,' she continued. 'It was Robbie Williams' "Angels", "Dance With My Father Again" by Luther Vandross and "Home" by Michael Bublé. As I was listening to them I was getting more and more emotional.'

She added, 'And the funny thing was, as I was doing this

I was thinking about Mary. I think it was a sign of something, I don't know what.'

When I told her that I'd had exactly the same experience her face just froze. We both knew that something had been going on this morning. The question was: what?

When we got to the centre, we found the other members of the class gathered there, including Mary.

'I've been thinking about you on the way over here,' I told her. 'And so has Anna.'

'Oh yes, why was that?' she asked.

'Oh, I'll tell you afterwards,' I said, mindful of the fact that it was time to start the class. 'It's a long story.'

The class had been going for about twenty minutes when I noticed Mary fishing her mobile phone out of her bag. When she saw the text message her face turned ashen. She immediately got up and grabbed her bag and coat.

'I'm really sorry, I've got to go,' she whispered, doing her best not to disturb the class.

The class went on for another three quarters of an hour or so. As we broke up, I headed downstairs to the reception to ask about Mary.

'Where did she have to go in such a rush?' I asked our receptionist at the time, Pat.

Pat looked at me with a grim expression. 'Her husband had just texted on her mobile in a terrible state. He had just found his father, lying dead in his living room. They think he had a massive heart attack and died, just like that.'

I was terribly upset for Mary. I knew she was from a tightly-knit family. The loss would have been devastating for them.

But almost immediately my thoughts began to return to the journey here in the car this morning. It all made sense now.

The spirit world had been giving both me and Anna a sign, one that I could now see we were meant to pass on to Mary. There was no doubt about it. The clues were unmistakeable; I just had to go through the songs: 'Angels', 'Dance With My Father Again' and 'Home'. They all added up to a sign that a father figure was passing over to spirit.

'What time did this happen?' I asked.

'They reckon he died at ten-thirty this morning.'

That had been the exact time that Anna and I had both pulled into the car park, both crying our eyes out at the music we'd been listening to.

When I next saw Mary I told her about what had happened. By now her father-in-law's funeral had taken place. She smiled and nodded as I explained the sequence of songs and the timing. She understood exactly what it meant and drew enormous comfort from it.

It didn't lessen the loss her husband and in-laws were feeling. But it did provide her – and hopefully them – with the knowledge that his existence was continuing, that he had found another place to call home.

Raymond's Way

Making a conscious connection between this world and the spirit realm is the key to understanding and using signs. If something happens, you need to be clear that the event really has a psychic or spiritual significance. Once you know that, you can then keep an eye out for that particular sign again and again. Then, each time it comes into your life, you will know that it signifies the spirit realm is close.

Often the sign will take the form of something that you already associate with the loved one who has passed over, such as a favourite song or movie, a meal or an animal. But sometimes it will not be. Sometimes it might be something quite surprising. It might even be something that your loved one actually disliked during their time here.

A good example of this occurred when I did an intimate psychic evening at a Marriott hotel in Swindon. These evenings were really nice affairs with a restricted audience of only 150 people. In a smaller room like that it's a much more pleasant and warm experience. Everyone can see each other and relate to each other and what's happening. It's not like performing in front of 1,000 people in a theatre. I really enjoy doing smaller events. You also get to know the people who have come along on a more personal level.

Among those attending this particular evening were a mother and daughter, Jackie and Barbara. They had come along, hoping to make a connection with Raymond, Jackie's husband and Barbara's dad, who hadn't passed over long before. He didn't come through that evening, as it happens. But they stayed behind afterwards to ask me to sign a book.

Jackie was a very sweet lady. She held my hand and said how much she'd enjoyed the evening and how pleased she was for those who had received messages. This to me confirmed what a great audience they had been. You don't always hear such sentiments when you sit down and meet people at the end of a show. I've encountered individuals who have stormed up to me and blamed me for ruining their nights because I hadn't brought through a loved one for them. When I see the negativity and anger inside them, I'm not surprised the spirits haven't wanted to talk to them for very long.

Jackie was the polar opposite of this. Over a drink, we chatted for a few minutes. She explained that her husband had passed from cancer in the past six months. She admitted she'd struggled during the first few months but that Barbara in particular had helped bring her through.

Raymond wasn't the sort of man to sit around and mope, apparently. He had been a successful businessman, with a lot of what my dad used to call get-up-and-go. He wouldn't have approved of her sitting in the house in the dark, crying. He would have wanted her to get on with her life.

I explained that the combination of her intense grief and his newness to the spirit world might have been the reason he hadn't come through that evening. But I assured her that if she kept his memory alive and perhaps occasionally spoke to him, he would deliver her a sign of his presence.

'He will show you something that will validate the fact that he is around you,' I told her. 'It could be that you hear a song that he used to sing to you. It could be that someone walks past you with the heavy scent of his aftershave. The smell will bring back that connection. But if you ask for a sign, make it difficult for him – don't make it something too easy!'

Jackie was really appreciative. We spoke in all for about ten minutes before I had to mingle a bit more with the rest of the audience. They were equally nice.

As the evening drew to a close, Jackie and Barbara came back to say goodbye. I wished them well and told them to let me know when Raymond showed himself. They promised to do so.

And then something wonderful happened.

They were walking to the door when I suddenly heard the phrase 'I did it my way' in my head. I didn't sense the presence of Jackie's husband Raymond at all. It felt like someone very different from the man they had described.

As the message intensified, I couldn't work out if the spirits were trying to show me the name 'Frank' or 'Frank Sinatra' or lead me in a different direction. But I knew it was meant for Jackie, so I shouted at her to come back.

'Why am I hearing Frank Sinatra singing "My Way"?' I asked Jackie.

She looked slightly unsure at first. 'Well, it was a song that he had very mixed feelings about,' she said. 'The last time I remember hearing it with Ray was at his best friend's funeral, which took place three months before Ray died, too. His friend's name was Frank,' she explained. 'Ray did what he always did when he heard it. He screwed up his face and said: "I really bloody hate this song!"'

The more I heard the more convinced I became that this was a sign from Raymond, a response to the request that Jackie, Barbara and I had put out to the spirit world. It resonated in several ways, not just because he disliked the song. The lyrics seemed to apply to Raymond in a very direct way. Jackie had already talked about how he was a really independent character, a man who did business on his terms, in his way. The song could have been written with him in mind.

By now I had a strong sense that this message was definitely being directed at Jackie and Barbara. 'OK. It may not have been his song, but I think this is the song that is going to be your sign that he is around,' I said. 'Listen out for it. I have a feeling you will hear it a lot more than you'd expect.'

Barbara and Jackie stayed in touch with me via email and came to see me again at another demonstration I did in the West Country. Again, they came to see me at the end of the show.

They told me that in the days, weeks and months after that night in Swindon, they had heard Frank Sinatra's 'My Way' time and time again.

'When I think about him, it comes on the radio,' Jackie told me. 'It's amazing.'

It reinforced my belief that spirits connect with us in subtle and sometimes unexpected ways – and that we must be aware of this. We may expect them to communicate via the safe and familiar. But they may also show themselves in very unfamiliar and surprising ways.

So it had proved with Raymond, a man who – in this life and the next – had always done it his way.

A Knock on the Wall

A lady called Natalie contacted me with a lovely story about her husband. She had lost him eighteen months earlier but regularly spoke to him, often last thing at night before she went to sleep.

One night she asked him for a sign that he was still around. 'Do something obvious, so I know it has to be you,' she said.

Later on that night she was woken up by the sound of knocking on one of the bedroom walls. There was a pattern to the knocking. It was five knocks then a gap, five knocks and then a gap. She was still half asleep and was confused at first.

She lived in a detached house. The walls didn't connect to another home, so it couldn't have been a neighbour banging on the wall. Suddenly she remembered the request she'd made to her husband before falling asleep. She was excited at the prospect of it being him but wasn't one hundred per cent convinced. So she spoke to him once more. 'OK, you can stop now,' she said.

The knocking stopped immediately.

Natalie thought this was absolutely fantastic. She had experienced some other strange things that she felt might have been a sign from her husband. But the knocking on the wall was by far the most dramatic. 'And the most comforting too,' she told me.

Sign Language: Listen to the Voices

One of the earliest clues I was given about my gift for connecting with the Other Side came in the form of voices that I could hear in my thoughts. On a couple of occasions they steered me away from situations that could have been dangerous for me.

When I was a teenager, for instance, a deep, disembodied voice once warned me against approaching a seedy-looking man in a car who had stopped to ask me for directions. I'd been walking towards him when the voice appeared. I listened to it and ran away just as the man lurched at me as he climbed out of the car. It later turned out he was a serial sex offender who was known to the police. Heaven only knows what would have happened if I'd ignored the voices.

They were able to offer more positive advice too. Early in my career I had been agonising over whether to hire a public hall to run my own circle. But then I'd heard a voice telling me, 'If you build it they will come.'

It was, of course, a line from the Kevin Costner film *Field of Dreams*, about a farmer who hears voices telling him to build a baseball pitch on his land in the middle of nowhere. He built it and in the end people did come to it.

The same happened with my class. I hired the hall and people came. More than a decade later, some of them still come each week to sit in circle with me.

Ever since then that phrase has been a very powerful message for me from spirit. If I hear someone repeat it in a conversation I know that it is a sign. For example, a friend of mine, Becky, said it to me while I was still deliberating over whether to move into the Dragonfly Centre that I now run in Waltham Abbey.

'Tracy, if you build it they will come,' she said.

It was just what I'd needed to hear at that time. It reinforced the feeling I had that I was doing the right thing. It was a really positive sign.

11 | Numbers

I've always had an interest in numbers and the part they play in shaping our fates. For a long time, it was purely an instinctive thing. Like most people, I suspect, I believed I had a lucky number. In my case it has always been the number nine, which has always been good for me, ever since I was a young girl. However, until recently I hadn't really connected numbers with my mediumship. I had never considered that the spirit world might use them to guide us.

But then I met my friend, the French numerologist Didier Boyer, who this book is dedicated to and who I have mentioned earlier. He changed my understanding of the power of numbers for ever. And he showed me that, as well as other physical phenomena, I should also look for numerical signs from the spirit world.

Didier and I worked together on a small television station called Destiny TV. We appeared on television together, on shows like *Richard and Judy* where I would make predictions using my psychic skills and he would do the same using numbers.

I loved Didier. He was this quirky little Frenchman. He loved his wine and he loved his rugby. He also liked the ladies and did very well with them. He was a good-looking man. He was very eccentric. He always carried a giant crystal wherever he went. He knew we all thought he was crazy for carrying it around with him but he didn't give a stuff.

He was absolutely passionate about numerology, a discipline that has been around in one form or another for a very long time. Ancient civilisations in the Middle East relied heavily on numbers in order to make their decisions and provide prophecies. Chinese culture, too, has for centuries associated particular numbers with particular qualities.

Didier, however, had brought the study into the modern world. He had come up with a comprehensive guide that told you what your own personal numbers were and how to use those numbers to guide you in life. He was a real original and a brilliant man.

He did my numbers soon after we first met. It was one of the most memorable – and slightly embarrassing – readings I've ever known. He sat me down and went through a process which produced my numerologically important numbers. They didn't include my lucky number nine, although he said I should carry on regarding it as important if I felt that way.

Instead they included numbers that made Didier very excited. In his distinctive French accent he told me I was a seven, eleven and twenty-two. He also said something I shall never forget. He told me that to be those numbers, as far as he was concerned, was a numerologist's orgasm!

What he meant by this was that seven, eleven and twenty-two have particularly powerful meanings. For instance, eleven is a number that is associated with not just mediums but people with powerful spiritual presences and charisma. This isn't always a good thing, Didier told me. There is such a thing as a 'negative eleven', which explains why other people linked to the number range from Jesus Christ, Barack Obama, Bill Clinton, Napoleon, Leonardo da Vinci, Mozart and David Beckham to Adolf Hitler.

In my particular case he said eleven told him a lot about my being an empathetic and sympathetic person. The fact that I also have the number twenty-two was, he told me, the most exciting thing about me.

On the one hand, the fact that I had twenty-two in my chart meant I probably had a tough early life with 'very tough lessons learned about my limitations'. That was certainly true. But it was the fact that – unusually – I had eleven and twenty-two together that had given him his 'numerologist's orgasm'.

According to Didier, people with eleven and twenty-two are somehow 'blessed'. The Dalai Lama has this combination, apparently. This blessing can sometimes feel like a curse, which again was definitely the case with me. I have often wished I wasn't gifted with psychic and mediumistic abilities. But the good news in my case, according to Didier anyway, was that I had a combination of facets that meant I was going to be an ambassador for the spirit world.

Given that he told me this soon after I'd taken a gamble on opening my own spiritual centre, I was very happy to hear it. It gave me an important boost at a time when I had plenty of doubts about what I was doing.

I was so impressed – and surprised – by Didier's reading that I have used his advice ever since. Along with nine, the numbers seven, eleven and twenty-two have been crucial in decisions I've made. And they have always guided me towards happy outcomes.

About four years ago, for example, I was looking for a new car. I had saved up the cash for it and wanted something decent, not an old banger. I'd come across a rather nice Ford that was on sale with a small, local garage. They had offered me such a good deal on it that I had begun to think: 'Don't rush in here; this is too good to be true.' So I sent out the thought to the spirit world that I'd like a sign.

The guy from the garage texted me the following morning to ask me if I was still interested in the car. If I wasn't, he was going to sell it on. He had another person interested, so he needed to know by lunchtime that day.

I knew it was time to 'put up or shut up', but was worried that I hadn't received a sign guiding me one way or the other. But then I looked at the time he had sent his message to me from the garage. It was eleven minutes past nine. Perfect. That was it, decision made.

I immediately called him back and agreed to the deal on the car. It turned out to be the ideal car for my needs and ran really well throughout the time I had it. I didn't regret buying it for a second, which was more than could be said for a few other cars I've owned in my time.

I told Didier about this and he laughed. 'Of course it worked,' he said. 'You used your numbers.'

It gave me the confidence to use my numbers more and more. Today, I will always numerologically check out my numbers before making big decisions. So for instance, I now live at a house which is number thirty-eight. I'd liked the house when I'd first seen it but needed to know it works in terms of numbers. Didier told me that I had to look at numbers laterally at times. It didn't take me long to see it: add three and eight together and you get an eleven. So that, again, was decision made.

I had a similar thing with my office, which is number nine on its street. Again that is compatible with my numbers. Both the places where I spend my life are connected to my most important numbers.

Numbers have moulded some of the biggest decisions I've made. Recently I was offered a chance to extend the premises at my centre. Another building next door had become available. I made sure that I exchanged contracts on a day that was numerologically good for me. My solicitors didn't know this, obviously, but I worked it out so that I signed on 11 September, a date that has bad connotations for other people now, but which for me is numerologically a good combination. The solicitors were pushing for me to delay to the twelfth or thirteenth, but I told them it had to be the eleventh or I wasn't going to sign.

Using my numbers makes me feel stronger about things. It can do the same for everyone, I believe. We are all being guided by the spirit world. I don't believe they are telling us what to do, but I do believe there is guidance that is available from the spirit world if you ask for it. I now believe firmly that numbers are one form of guidance.

However, as with other signs, you have to use them responsibly and for the right reasons. For instance, the spirit world is not going to give you the numbers that will win you the lottery.

There is a very good reason for this: no one should have that amount of money as it unbalances and interferes with the natural order of things. If someone wins the lottery they might stop doing what they are meant to be doing; they might stop going down their life's path. I know that if I'd won the lottery when I was thirty then I wouldn't be doing what I'm doing now. I wouldn't have fought to get where I am today. The spirit world doesn't want that. So it doesn't help in decisions like that.

Sign Language: A Quick Guide to Numerology and the Main Numbers

A numerologist will use your date of birth to look at two key numbers: your destiny number and your expression number. These show what your purpose is in life and how your personality will allow you to fulfil it.

Lots of numerologists have different ways of working but the easiest way of finding your life path number, for instance, is simply to add up the digits of your date of birth and then add up the digits of the number this produces. So, for instance, if you were born on 2 January 1964, then your life path number is five. (2+1+1+9+6+4 = 23, then 2+3 = 5). Each number has different properties. It tells you about your life path but it also tells you about your personality.

One

Because it is the first number, one is considered to have great power. But it is also associated with ego, wanting to be the centre of attention, literally being 'number one'. The life path of someone with one in their numbers is summed up by independence and being an individual. A person with one in their numbers can be dynamic and charismatic, but equally they can be selfish and melodramatic.

Two

Two is a sign of peace and harmony. It's about partnerships and interacting with others. Someone with two in their numbers is more likely to achieve things as part of a team rather than as an individual. It is also a feminine number and signifies the protective side of our nature. In a negative way, this can make someone over-protective.

Three

This is a number associated with creativity and self-expression so it is commonly linked to people who are writers, actors and artists. It is considered a lucky number too. On the negative side, it can be a sign of someone who takes unnecessary risks or who is pessimistic. On the positive side it is associated with wisdom, understanding and a great sense of humour.

Four

Four is linked to patience and a practical nature. People with this in their numbers have a talent for organisation and hard work. It is also associated with the earth, so people associated with four tend to be down-to-earth characters. But they can also have another side to them and be independent, structured thinkers.

Five

The life path of someone with five in their numbers is associated with adventure and freedom. People with this number will grow by trying lots of different experiences. It also represents an analytical nature, someone who thinks through their problems, but sometimes over-thinks. Five is a sign that determines our intellectual ability as well as our mental health. People with five in their numbers may live life to the limit.

Six

Six is a caring number. People with this in their numbers may follow a life path that is about compassion and caring for other people. It is considered the 'mother and father number'. Six is also associated with beauty and harmony. It is also about tact and being able to talk to anyone, so people with six in their numbers make good diplomats. On the negative side, six can be linked to jealousy and vengefulness.

Seven

Seven is a sign of an inward-looking and intellectual mind. People with this number think about life deeply and like to be left alone to do so. It is strongly associated with the spiritual and secrets that need to be uncovered. It is thought to be a sacred number. This number is linked to ancient wisdom that claims the earth was created in seven days, the kabbalah has seven spirits and the ancient solar system was made up of seven luminaries. People with seven in their numbers are associated with psychic abilities too.

Eight

Someone with eight as their life path number is defined by the search for material success. They are also associated with persistence and business and financial skills. Eight is also associated with hard work and learning through experience, and can mean that life is full of big setbacks.

Nine

Having nine as your life path number means you have a compassionate and humanitarian nature. You are associated with idealism and helping others. Ancient cultures regarded nine as a sacred number. It is also associated with change and inspiration. Inventors are commonly associated with the number nine.

Zero

Zero is associated with great and sometimes profound transformations in life. It is a very intense number and is used carefully by numerologists.

Eleven, Twenty-two and Thirty-three

These three numbers are regarded as the master numbers. Having these numbers in your chart is regarded as being very auspicious.

12 | Rainbows and Other Natural Phenomena

Spirits can manifest themselves in the elements around us. Often they are present in the wind and the rain, the sun and the sky. As Elizabeth Frye's famous poem 'Do Not Stand At My Grave And Weep' says: 'I am in a thousand winds that blow/I am the softly falling snow/I am the gentle showers of rain/I am the fields of ripening grain.' These nature signs are often some of the most beautiful and memorable signs of all.

Over The Rainbow

There is a real resonance to rainbows as a symbol of our transient nature. Many regard the sight of a rainbow as something very spiritual. Perhaps it is because a rainbow symbolises a bridge to somewhere else. We don't quite know where it leads. But we have a feeling that it is somewhere that makes us feel more peaceful and safe.

I certainly regard it as a powerful sign, and have met many people for whom rainbows hold a very special significance. I don't think, for instance, it's a coincidence that the song 'Somewhere Over The Rainbow' as sung by the tragic Eva Cassidy has become a very popular song at funerals. I can see why – it is very evocative, both in terms of its lyrics but also the beauty of the song, her voice and the sadness of her life.

Cassidy dreamed of success but never saw it in this life. She was a struggling musician, playing to half-empty clubs and bars for much of her career. Yet soon after her passing she became world famous with her albums reaching Number One. She had passed over, but her music lived on. People are very moved by that.

Her song was particularly resonant for one mother, who I got to know well. Her name was Cathey and she had lost her son at the tender age of seven. After a long fight, he had died of a brain tumour.

Cathey had devoted the final months of his life to caring for him in the most extraordinary way. She virtually lived in the hospital ward where he was being cared for and regularly slept on an inflatable mattress at the bottom of his bed. She had been with him almost every waking moment during his long, slow deterioration.

I read for her a few months after his passing and was able to connect him to her. As I did so, I began to appreciate the extraordinary role she'd played in his life.

The boy's name was Timothy. He showed me his final moments in this life. His mother was with him, of course. As he was passing into spirit, she was stroking his hair. She was lying on an inflatable mattress next to his bed at the time. And she was doing a guided meditation for him. She was trying to ease his path. So she was saying things such as 'go to the water, go to the river, go into the garden'. I really don't know how she had found the strength because I wouldn't have been able to do it if it was one of my sons about to go, but as I saw this I thought that she was doing something really beautiful.

She said, 'Look for the rainbow.' And as she said that he passed over. So they used the song 'Somewhere Over the Rainbow' at his funeral.

And now rainbows have a special significance for Cathey. Her younger children draw rainbows, for instance. They are too young to know that there is a connection – her daughter was still a baby when Timothy passed over. So whenever they draw one, Cathey knows it is a sign.

For Cathey, the sign doesn't have to come in the form of a physical rainbow. It can be a painting of a rainbow, or something with the word 'rainbow' on it. It could be a ceramic rainbow. It could even be a song by the band Rainbow.

Cathey now draws enormous strength from every sight of a rainbow that she comes across. Indeed, a rainbow had even helped her when she'd come to see me. She told me that she'd been nervous about seeing me and had even thought of turning round and not coming into my centre. But then, as she'd been about to turn on her heel, she saw a sign in my window. It was for a natural healer who works here. She calls her service 'Rainbow Therapy'. And on the front of her flyer was an image of the seven colours arching through the sky.

Cathey doesn't need to chase after rainbows. They come to her . . .

The Rainbow Bridge

I was on stage in a theatre in the West Country one night when a message came through from the spirit of a mother who had recently passed over. Her name was Jane and she was looking to connect with her son, Richie.

It turned out Richie was in the audience with his wife, Debbie. Within minutes he had recognised his mother from the information I provided. He became quite emotional when he realised it was her. It was clear to me they must have been very close. In the weeks and months since her passing he had clearly suffered a great deal.

His mother told him that she was glad he had just got back from a good holiday. 'Your mother is telling me that she was so pleased you and Debbie were able to get away for a fortnight and have some peace,' I said. He nodded at this. 'I know you have been through a lot and it lifted the load for you.'

His mother was a very warm and bright presence. For a minute or two all I could see in my head was a fantastic, brilliantly coloured rainbow, forming over a bridge of some kind. I also had the music from Eva Cassidy's version of 'Somewhere Over The Rainbow' playing in my head.

When I mentioned the song Richie started crying. 'We played that at my mother's funeral,' he said.

His mother wanted to be more specific though. 'Your mother is telling me that she saw you watching that rainbow on the bridge,' I told him.

He looked shocked at this.

I continued, 'And she knows that when you looked later

at the image you'd captured of it on your camera you thought of her.' I explained, 'Richie, your mother wants you to know that it was a sign from her. It was a sign that she will always be around you, wherever you go.'

Richie and Debbie came up to see me after the show and explained that he had, indeed, taken a photograph of a rainbow when they'd been on holiday. They had gone to Venice to celebrate Debbie's birthday but also to get over the trauma of the funeral.

The weather had been beautiful but one afternoon there had been this sudden and unexpected deluge. As the skies had cleared, Richie and Debbie had been walking across a bridge when they had seen this absolutely perfect rainbow forming in the grey skies above the lagoon. Richie had thought of his mother immediately. And he'd taken a photograph to remember both her and the moment.

'It's funny,' he said. 'I did have this strange feeling as I was standing there, that she was somewhere around me.' And it turns out she was . . .

Looking up to the Heavens

Signs can manifest themselves everywhere and in the most unexpected – and sometimes beautiful – ways. One of the most gorgeous descriptions of a sign I've heard was from a friend who is active within the Spiritualist Church movement.

A few years ago she had been due to attend a meeting of the Spiritualist Church in the town of Gravesend in Kent. It was some way from her home so the night before she had stayed as a guest in the home of a prominent member of the church.

Her host, a very nice lady by all accounts, lived in a lovely country home, with a beautiful garden and a large conservatory. On the morning of the service, my friend had sat down to have breakfast with the lady and they started chatting. The conversation had turned, perhaps understandably, to their beliefs and their individual experiences within the Spiritualist movement.

My friend had started talking about her pathway into the movement. But soon after she began describing her journey she began to hear a voice, whispering quietly. It kept saying simply: 'Look up to the sky, look up to the sky.'

Sitting as she was inside a large, glass conservatory this was easily done. She simply looked up through the glass ceiling at the clear blue sky. As she did so, she was overwhelmed by what she saw in the heavens above.

A huge, white cross had formed in the clouds. It was, she recalled later, absolutely beautiful.

Her hostess noticed her looking up and glanced upwards herself. She too was spellbound by what she saw. The two of them sat there staring at the formation for at least half an hour as it hovered overhead. Eventually the cloud began moving very slowly in the sky, retaining its shape all the time.

Both women were quite moved by the experience. They knew it wasn't a man-made phenomenon created, for instance, by the vapours of two planes intersecting. There was no obvious, rational explanation for it, in scientific terms. What it was, of course, was a sign. These were perfectly formed clouds that had appeared overhead – at the precise moment the two women were discussing their faith.

Signs like that don't need too much examination. They defy doubt and should simply be enjoyed in all their wonder. That is precisely how my friend now looks back at the moment. She calls it very simply: 'One of the very best things that has ever happened to me.' Her faith, naturally, remains as strong as ever.

13 | Visions and Dreams

The most dramatic way in which spirits manifest themselves, of course, are in visions. This is where their physical form can appear to be in the room with us. Visions can appear to us all at any time of the day or night. But they do tend to occur at night-time, usually when we are asleep or in that semi-conscious state that we enter as we wake up.

There is a very good reason why spirits find it easier to connect with us when we are in this condition. When we are in a dream state the waves of our brains are in what is known as a 'theta rhythm'. When a medium is connecting to the spirit world, their brain too is in this state. It brings them closer to the energy and vibration of the spirit world. So it is no surprise that during those periods when we are fully asleep or even in a semi-sleep state, we find ourselves more open to signs from the afterlife.

I have come across countless examples of this during my career and have noticed that the signs people receive in these circumstances are often extremely vivid and potent.

The Thirteenth Night

One of the most powerful visions I've heard of appeared to a very close friend of mine, Michelle. A few years ago, Michelle went through a terrible time. Her husband Greg was diagnosed with terminal cancer. He was only in his forties.

Michelle and Greg had been a really happy couple. They had done everything together. For Michelle, watching Greg slowly fade from this life was a horrendous experience.

However, Michelle had been able to draw strength from the fact that Greg was a very spiritual man. He believed absolutely in the afterlife and had been adamant that he would return to see Michelle after he had passed over. He talked very openly about it. He even gave her specific timing.

'I'm coming back on the thirteenth night,' he told her. 'I don't want you to look for me, or ask for me, or try to smell me, or anything like that before the thirteenth night.'

At the time Michelle hadn't really taken his promise very seriously at all. She took the view that if it was helping Greg deal with his illness then it was fine.

That view changed somewhat after Greg passed over.

The aftermath of his death was a real succession of disasters. First, Michelle had real problems getting Greg's body released from the hospital. Her doctor was away on holiday and was unable to complete the death certificate. Then, there was a further delay because of the weekend.

Eventually it took twelve days to get his funeral organised. The night before he was due to be buried, his coffin was brought home. As Greg lay in the open coffin, Michelle, their children and Greg's friends and family were able to pay their last respects to him. It was, obviously, a very, very emotional evening.

When everyone had left, Michelle went to bed and fell asleep quickly, exhausted. In the middle of the night she was woken up by the sound of crying. She immediately thought it was one of the children and got up to head to their bedrooms. But as she adjusted to the light in her room, she saw a figure sitting on the edge of her bed crying. To her amazement she saw it was Greg.

He was only there briefly and they didn't speak. But she was overwhelmed to see him. She immediately ran downstairs to the still open coffin. When she looked inside she saw tears had formed in the corners of his eyes.

It was only then that she realised it was the thirteenth night since his death. He had returned to see her exactly as he had promised.

Pulling the Plug

My friend, Linda, experienced several strange events in the months following the death of her son. Each had made her more and more convinced of his presence in the spirit world.

The first was a curious feeling. Every now and again she would feel a strange energy in the top part of her body and in her arms in particular. It was hard for her to describe – it didn't feel like anything she'd felt before. It felt as if someone was standing behind her. She suspected it was the spirit of her son but couldn't really be sure.

It was around the same time that her dog began behaving strangely, running to and barking at the front door of her house all the time. Each time he charged off she would head to the front of the house to check out what was causing the fuss. Each time, however, there had been nobody there.

Intriguing as these manifestations were, they didn't convince her that her son's spirit had safely crossed over to the Other Side. It took another event – this time a sign – to finally persuade her of the truth.

Her son was her firstborn child. In addition she had three small children so her hectic and demanding life meant that she was, understandably, exhausted by the end of most days. On this particular night she had gone to bed feeling utterly drained. She'd been certain that she was going to fall into a deep and long sleep the second her head hit the pillow. But she didn't.

For some strange reason, as she lay in bed all she could see when she shut her eyes was the plug at the back of her television downstairs. No matter what she tried to do, she couldn't get rid of it. She tried reading for a bit, then lay there reciting lists to herself. She tried everything but to no avail. All she could think about was the plug.

She knew what her head was telling her to do. She didn't normally disconnect the plug. Normally the television remained on standby all night. But she knew that something – or someone – was telling her to pull out the plug tonight.

She was aware it made no sense but in the end she

became so furious about not being able to get to sleep that she threw back the duvet, climbed out of bed and trotted downstairs to the living room to do what she realised she had to do.

With the plug safely removed from the wall she wearily climbed back up the stairs and got back under the duvet. This time, the minute she hit the pillow she was asleep. She slept like a log.

The following morning after giving the children breakfast she went back into the living room to put in the plug so that they could watch some television. The instant she did so and flicked the switch back on there was a loud and very scary bang. Fuses were blown and it took an electrician to come out to fix the problem. He said there was a fault in the wiring around the switch. It had been an accident waiting to happen.

When she told him that she normally left it on overnight but had disconnected it the previous night he gave her a puzzled look.

'That might have saved you from something serious,' he said. 'This wiring was ready to go any minute. It could easily have started a fire last night.'

Linda felt relieved at first. But then she felt really overwhelmed. Something – or someone – had forced her to remove that plug the night before. Something – or someone – may have saved her life and the lives of her three children, too.

She remains convinced that it was a sign from the afterlife, and most probably from her son himself.

Crossing the Road

Spirits can manifest themselves in our dreams. They can appear in all sorts of forms. And they can issue us with all sorts of advice and information about what is going on in our lives. There are times when they can also warn us about the future. Often, these dreams come in quite dramatic form.

So it was with a lady called Joanne. Joanne was a busy young mother who, like so many of us, was constantly trying to juggle her life.

Deep down, I think all of us worry about whether we are doing a good job in keeping it all together. I know it was something I lost sleep over when I was a young mother. I had plenty of bad dreams about the job I was doing as a mother for my sons James and Ryan.

Joanne's dream was of a similar nature. The difference was, however, that it was actually a sign from the spirit world – a warning of events that were about to unfold. Joanne recounted the dream to me some time later, but it was still as vivid in her mind as if it had happened half an hour ago.

She had dreamed that she was collecting her daughter, Alex, from school. She had pulled up in her car on the other side of the road from the school gates. She had just opened the door to get out when she felt herself being drawn back into the car.

It turned out that Joanne's brother-in-law, Christy, who had passed over to the Other Side several years earlier, was sitting in the car alongside her. She had been delighted to see him and had been chatting away merrily to him, catching up on all sorts of family news.

Joanne had become so engrossed in her conversation with Christy that she had completely forgotten about her daughter, who had been standing on the opposite side of the road, waiting for her mother to collect her and guide her safely back to the car. Before she knew it, Alex had stepped out into the road ready to cross over to the car.

Joanne described to me what happened next in minute detail. 'I couldn't get to her but I was shouting at her, calling her name,' she remembered.

Then, out of nowhere, a white van appeared.

Joanne saw her daughter remain fixed to the spot in the middle of the road. Alex didn't know what to do – run back to the pavement or towards her mother in the car. The speeding van was within an inch of hitting her daughter when Joanne suddenly woke up.

Joanne was so shaken by the dream that it stayed with her well after she'd got up the next day. As was her usual routine, she dropped her daughter off at school that morning and then popped in to see her parents. Her father was due to collect Alex at the end of the day while Joanne went to an appointment.

Over a cup of tea she told her parents about her dream and how shaken it had left her. She'd then headed off to work, promising to see her parents and Alex in the evening.

When Joanne arrived at her parents' house eight or so hours later she found her father in a terrible state. He had been barely able to speak he was so shaken up. He was still visibly trembling.

It had been her mother who had explained what had happened when he'd turned up to collect Alex earlier that afternoon.

Her dad had turned up at school right on time, as the pupils were emptying out of the classrooms. As was the usual routine, he had parked on the other side of the road on the understanding that he would cross to collect Alex and then bring her safely back to the car. But today as he pulled up, opened the door and got ready to climb out, he saw Alex was already standing on the edge of the kerb looking animatedly at the traffic.

Before he could do anything she had stepped out into the road.

It must have taken a millisecond for his brain to work out what was happening. Suddenly, out of the corner of his eye he saw a white van speeding down the road, seemingly oblivious to the child in the road ahead of it.

Joanne's father shouted out Alex's name. She froze to the spot, suddenly aware that a van was heading towards her. Before she could do anything, however, her grandfather had scooped her up and carried her back to the pavement. He had shot out of the car, run across the road only a few yards in front of the approaching white van and rescued his granddaughter.

As her mother retold the story, her father was sitting quietly, nodding. Eventually he managed to speak. 'If you hadn't told me about that dream about Christy, I wouldn't have moved so fast,' he said. 'Another second or two and that van would have hit her, and with the speed it was doing that would have been the end of her.'

Joanna still talks about the events of that afternoon now, several years later. She is convinced that, had her brother-in-law not appeared in her dream, she would not have passed on the warning to her father and he would never have acted as quickly and decisively as he did.

'I thanked Christy afterwards because I think he saved her life that day,' she told me. 'But don't tell my dad – he thinks he did!'

14 | Multiple Signs

In life there are people who are more communicative than others. Some have the gift of the gab while others do not. So it is in the spirit world as well.

As we have seen, spirits can speak to us in an infinite number of ways. They can appeal to our senses. They can make use of technology and the physical world around us. They can manifest themselves in every conceivable form. If we think of the types of signs they give us as different languages, then the spirits are multi-lingual. They speak to us in a myriad different ways.

Some people seem to be able to send multiple signs to their loved ones from the Other Side. They show their ongoing presence by influencing all sorts of seemingly minor events in the lives of those they have left behind. I've encountered a few examples of spirits like this over the years. One that will always stick in my mind is that of Tony, a father whose daughter contacted me in the months after his passing.

The Five-Pound Note
Tony sounded like a real character, a larger-than-life guy.

He had a huge number of friends and had lived a colourful life. He had, among other things, been a very good rock drummer and a collector of sporting memorabilia. He was clearly a man with a real lust for life.

According to his daughter, Tony had passed quite suddenly but had begun to show signs of his new existence in the spirit world almost immediately. Before his funeral, for instance, the family had been debating which piece of music to play in the church. Tony had played on a few records and they wanted something that reflected his love of the drums and of music in general. After much agonising they chose a song that he had played drums on many years earlier, but they still hadn't been sure about the choice.

A few weeks after the funeral, a family member went through some of Tony's personal affairs and found a letter. Tony wasn't a great one for putting down his thoughts, but in this note he had described how the song that had been played at his funeral had been his all-time favourite. He was particularly proud of it because he was the only drummer ever to have recorded it.

When the letter came to light the family were delighted. They were also convinced that Tony had somehow led them to making the right choice. This was because by that time all sorts of other strange things had begun to happen which suggested that Tony was sending them messages from the Other Side.

On one occasion, the family had organised a tribute night to remember Tony. As part of the night they held a raffle draw and sold five hundred tickets on behalf of charity. Tony had been the kind of guy who would always have a go at a raffle. In fact, Tony had won a raffle two weeks before he died. The prize had been a haircut and a range of hair products from a local hairdresser.

When the raffle draw was made during his tribute night, the main prize went to the hairdresser who had donated the prize Tony had won. Again, the family were convinced that Tony had organised it somehow.

All sorts of other things happened in the weeks following Tony's funeral. For instance, he definitely seemed to be able to influence the electrics in his home. When his daughter asked him to show himself by doing something with the lights, they began to flicker on and off for a full minute. At one point, every time his name was mentioned the doorbell at his home rang. Yet whenever someone went to the door they would discover that no one was there. In the end the family had to take the batteries out of the doorbell because everyone was getting so freaked out.

Things also began to disappear – and then reappear in curious ways. The night before Tony died he had bought his grandson a toy train. After his passing, the train went missing for a few weeks. His daughter had been frantic to find it and had turned the house upside down searching for it. Then one day, when she was cleaning her son's bedroom, it suddenly appeared in the middle of the rug. She was convinced Tony had put it there.

Similarly, his daughter had borrowed Tony's 'good hammer' from him months before he died. He had been pestering her to return it during his final days but she'd been completely unable to find it in her house. She'd looked everywhere with no luck. Yet two weeks after Tony's passing she walked into her bedroom and saw the hammer lying in the middle of the floor on the carpet. She couldn't believe it.

The most amazing thing of all, however, happened when Tony's son took a book containing all of his father's memorabilia to his local pub to show his mates. One of his father's most prized possessions was one of the limited edition Scottish Jack Nicklaus five-pound notes that were printed a few years ago. They are now collector's items worth much more than their face value.

As his friends pored over his dad's book, the son went to the bar to get a round of drinks. He paid and the barman gave him his change. It contained a Jack Nicklaus five-pound note.

Jack's Journey

Mediums believe that the transition into the life that begins after death is easier for people who have an understanding of the spirit world. Somehow, the fact that they are open and sensitive to the spirit dimension helps ease their journey. As a result, they are in a position to make contact from the Other Side, via messages and signs, much more quickly than other people.

If ever someone's passing proved that this is the case, it was that of a highly intelligent and gifted young man named Jack who died very recently. When Jack passed over, his parents, Lisa and Malcolm, endured what they called the hardest time of their lives. Jack had been an energetic, loving, young man with his life in front of him. His loss was a crippling blow to his parents and his whole family.

Yet, within days of his passing, the family began to see curious signs of his ongoing existence. The first one occurred after they had gone to see his body laid out. It was obviously an incredibly emotional moment. To make matters worse, it was Lisa's birthday.

After leaving the funeral directors, Lisa and Malcolm headed to a nearby beach. During the past few traumatic days, Lisa had often felt the urge to walk along the coastline and simply stare out to sea.

As they made their way there, they talked about what they needed to do in the difficult couple of days ahead. In the aftermath of Jack's passing, they had been trying to contact everyone who knew him to tell them the news.

One of his closest friends was his former mental-health nurse, Barry, but he had left the area and now lived thirty miles away. They had no way of contacting him and weren't in a state of mind to be able to search for him. As Lisa told me, simply getting out of bed was challenge enough in itself. Lisa and Malcolm were simply too heartbroken to try to do anything to find Barry. But once again, they wondered how they might reach him. They concluded that it was simply not going to be possible.

When they got to the coast, they made their way to a remote area of the beach. Even though it was October, the weather was warm and the day was still and sultry. As they walked along the water's edge, they saw that the only other people on the beach were leaving. They would soon have the place to themselves.

All of a sudden a jogger appeared in the distance, running with his earphones in place. For a second, Lisa thought she was going mad. She was sure it was Barry, so she told Malcolm to chase after him. However, Malcolm wasn't as fit as he once was and failed to catch up with the running man.

As Lisa and Malcolm sat down on a rocky outcrop they reasoned that the chances of Barry's running along that particular stretch of remote beach, many miles away from where he lived, at the precise moment they had arrived there were a billion to one at least. They sat there in what Lisa later described as the 'immense, debilitating sadness that only someone who has lost a child can understand'. She described it as feeling a pain 'so heavy and real it feels as if you will be crushed by its burden'.

The sun was setting by now and they were even more alone than before. But then, out of nowhere, the jogger they'd seen before suddenly appeared again. This time he headed straight towards them, at first oblivious of their presence. But as he got closer he began to slow down.

Eventually he came to a stop a few yards away from them. He took out his earphones and looked at them. 'Malcolm, Lisa, what brings you here? And how's Jack?'

Barry was shattered by the news they gave him. But he agreed to come to the funeral, along with another social worker who had cared for Jack.

Two months later the family had to deal with another

loss when a great-uncle of Lisa's, Cyril, passed over just before Christmas. As Lisa and Malcolm weren't relishing the prospect of spending Christmas at home so soon after Jack's passing, they decided to drive over to see Cyril's family on Christmas Day.

Inevitably their thoughts were once more dominated by their son. Finding it hard to deal with the pain once more, Lisa said out loud in the car: 'Uncle Cyril, if you are with Jack please give us a sign.'

Almost as soon as she said this, an object flew across the path of the car. It was a sky lantern. A few months earlier, Lisa and Malcolm wouldn't have known what it was. But when Jack died some friends had decided to light sky lanterns to remember him by – paper lanterns inscribed with loving words and wishes, which were then lit so that they floated up into the air. At the time, Lisa and Malcolm had been incredibly moved by the sight of them drifting off into the evening. And, in a reading with me, Jack had told his parents how much he'd loved the lanterns. 'Wow, they were all for me!' he'd exclaimed.

As they watched this lantern disappear on Christmas Day, Malcolm and Lisa were lifted up, too. Again, the chances of seeing one pass in front of their car as they were driving along were simply impossible to calculate. As Lisa says, she simply doesn't believe in coincidences like that. Once more they had been given a sign from the spirit world and Jack's place within it. It eased the pain of what was always going to be a difficult Christmas, making it just that little bit less hard to bear.

As the weeks went by, they heard stories from Jack's friends who had been sent signs of their own. Apparently, his brother and best friend were hanging out together one day, when they had unexpectedly found some Carling lager and pear cider sitting on a kitchen worktop – their favourite drinks, but there was no explanation of how the drinks had suddenly appeared there. Another friend received a message from Jack's phone days after his passing. It just said 'from Jack'. Again, his parents were dumbstruck by this. Since Jack's passing they hadn't used or even switched on Jack's phone. During those difficult, dark days, Jack – it seems – was on hand to offer all sorts of signs.

His mother had faced a terrible dilemma about whether to have Jack buried or cremated. He had always predicted he would be dead by the time he was twenty-five and had passed two years before that age, at only twenty-three. So he had talked a lot about the details of his funeral, from the songs he wanted played to the people he wanted to attend.

And yet, as she had faced the prospect of meeting his wishes, Lisa realised she didn't know one of the most important details of all. She finally called a family meeting at which his brother and sister said their feeling was that Jack wanted to be buried.

The decision made, Lisa felt relieved at having the responsibility removed from her. Along with her other children, she went up to Jack's room to find the music that they knew they would need for the funeral. He had a vast collection of vinyl records, tapes and CDs. As they went through them his brother noticed there was an LP on the turntable of Jack's record player. It was called, very simply, 'Burial'. His mother and siblings knew at that instant that they were doing exactly what he wanted.

The Two Brothers

As I know myself from the time of the death of my nan, the spirit world can bombard you with signs in the multiple languages of sound, sight and scent. I have also come across many other people and families who have experienced multiple signs in this way.

One of the most striking was the case of a middle-aged guy called Rory. Rory had lost his brother, Terry, in a mountaineering accident. Terry had fallen off a ledge while climbing in Snowdonia in north Wales.

The two brothers had always been very close. There was only a year between them in age and they'd been inseparable since boyhood. As grown men they had still watched football and gone to the pub together. The loss of Terry left Rory bereft – he had lost his brother and his best friend at the same time.

The tragedy had been felt all the way through the family. Terry had been a really vibrant life force within the family. His absence left a gaping void. Rory was a young granddad and even his grandchildren had been affected by the loss of their uncle Terry.

Because of the nature of the accident, it had taken three weeks for the body to be recovered, a formal inquest to be opened and for a funeral to be arranged. During that time, however, the family were given several signs that Terry was still around.

Rory's grandson had the first couple of experiences. A few days after Terry's passing he began to feel the temperature dropping around him whenever he was in his uncle's old house. Even more strangely, on two occasions he was standing inside the house, with all the doors and windows closed, when he felt a stiff breeze blowing past him. It was as if he was standing outside during a gale, he told his grandfather.

Then, on the day the family were getting together to plan Terry's funeral, one of the other grandchildren was getting into a car. It was a sunny day and the light was dazzling. When he looked at his own reflection in the tinted window, the little boy was shocked to see Terry standing behind him, smiling. He nearly jumped out of his skin, according to Rory.

The little boy's sister, Rory's granddaughter, experienced similar things. She was walking to school one day when she felt a gentle tugging at her raincoat. She turned around to see who it was, expecting to find it was her mother telling her off about something or other, as mums always do. But she saw that her mother had actually stopped twenty yards back down the road to talk to a friend. There was no one standing anywhere near her.

Then, one night, she saw a little girl standing at the bottom of her bed. When she described her to Rory and the rest of the family, some thought it sounded like the way Rory's mother, the little girl's great-grandmother, had looked when she was a little girl. This is often the case with spirits that appear to children. They too appear in child form.

During the run-up to Terry's funeral, the family had been talking about these events, yet Rory was sceptical. He heard all these things and dismissed them. He was a spiritual person, but he couldn't accept what he was being told. He put the events down to the children's over-active imaginations. Much as he wanted to see some evidence that his brother was still around, he simply didn't believe it.

But then he started experiencing things himself.

One night he was woken up in the small hours. As his eyes adjusted to the darkness, he saw the figure of a young man standing in the room, watching him intently. At first he was convinced someone had broken into the house. He was just working out what to do about it when the figure simply vanished into thin air.

Rory was completely freaked out by this experience and couldn't get back to sleep for ages. Eventually he did nod off, however, only to be woken up again. It was still dark outside, but the first twittering of the birds in the trees and a silver sliver of light in the window hinted at the coming dawn. Once again, the figure of the man was standing in the corner, surveying him with the look of a scientist studying some sort of rare sample. For a second, Rory thought it was a young Terry. But once more, he dissolved into thin air, this time before Rory could look at him properly.

This was just the beginning of a series of strange happenings in his house. Next, the telephone began ringing at odd hours, almost always in the dead of night. The same thing happened each time: the moment Rory picked it up the line went dead. When he dialled 1471 to check who it was there was no record of a call. It was odd in the extreme.

The strange events weren't confined to the night-time. Every now and again Rory was convinced he could feel someone brushing against him ever so lightly.

The final straw came when one day he was going through some old drawers in a chest in Terry's old living room. In one of them he found a faded old photograph of his brother smiling at him. 'Hello, mate,' he said, close to tears.

At that exact moment the television in the corner came on of its own accord. Rory checked the remote control to make sure nothing had pressed it accidentally, but it was on top of a bookshelf, out of reach.

There are moments when it becomes impossible to resist the evidence that the spirit world presents to us. There are times when surely even the most sceptical and doubting of us simply have to hold up our hands up and say – that can only have been the work of forces beyond this life.

When the television turned itself on like that, Rory finally accepted that his brother's presence continued to occupy the house. He had passed over into another existence. He wasn't around in the way that he had been. But he was around.

From then on Rory began speaking to Terry on a regular basis. The two brothers were reunited once more.

A Loving Touch

Spirits often use touch to make their presence felt. This can be the subtlest of signs. It might be the brushing of a cheek or the stroking of an arm. It might be a tingling sensation that you feel running down your body when you are in their presence.

It's a type of sign that I'm very familiar with myself. Both my grandparents have the ability to manifest themselves to me via touch. Since I sat with her in the chapel of rest and felt a wave of heat washing over me, my nan has let me know she is around by raising the temperature around me.

By contrast, my granddad, Stanley, lets me know he is present by making my nose itch ever so slightly. As I scratch it, I always say a quiet, inward hello.

Touch is, however, a very easy sign to dismiss or misunderstand. I have known many people who have felt a sensation in their arm and headed not for a medium but a doctor, worried they were having a heart attack. But I have also heard many heart-warming stories of those who have felt the reassuring presence of someone who has passed over manifest itself in a loving touch.

A young lad called Brendan told me about one of the loveliest examples of this that I've encountered. Brendan was quite a lonely, sensitive guy, even though he lived with his parents. He had a great interest in the psychic world and had taken some courses at my centre. I had been quite impressed by him. I felt he had a talent. One day Brendan told me about the experiences he had been having at home.

Brendan had been struggling with his emotions since losing his job and his long-term girlfriend in the space of a few months. But it was when he lost his beloved grandmother that he hit rock bottom. He admitted that he felt lost and rudderless in life. His grandma had been a real character – a strong, old-fashioned matriarch. And Brendan had been her favourite in the family. He missed her terribly. Yet, despite his interest in the afterlife, he couldn't convince himself that she had passed over to spirit and that her existence continued.

I suggested that he reach out to the spirit world and ask them for a sign from her. Typically, he asked me what to look out for. If I had a pound for every time I've been asked that I'd be the owner of a Premiership football club! I simply told him to keep an open heart and an open mind. 'Keep talking to your grandmother and something will happen, I'm sure,' I told him.

One night soon afterwards he went to bed after asking the spirit world for help. He was just drifting off to sleep, with his right arm down over the blanket and his left hand up at his face, when suddenly – seemingly out of nowhere – he felt a light stroking sensation running up and down his arm. It was dark, the lights were all out, but he could feel a distinct presence in the room.

Encouraged by this, he kept asking for signs. A few nights after that first incident, he was watching television when he felt an icy blast of cold air blow through the living room. His parents were in bed and all the doors and windows in the house were closed.

Again, he felt a presence accompanying the blast of air. It was almost as if someone was breathing heavily. He became convinced that spirits were present in the house, but he was still unsure whether it was his grandmother.

He put this thought out to the spirit world. Late one night, long after his parents had gone to bed, he went into the kitchen to make himself a drink. As he walked into the room he was hit by a strong, almost overwhelming smell of tobacco. It was as if someone had been smoking in the room. Neither he nor his parents had ever smoked cigarettes. The only member of his family who had smoked had been his grandmother, who used to roll her own Golden Virginia 'ciggies'.

The aroma in the kitchen reminded him of the pungent tobacco she used to keep in her little tin.

From then on Brendan was convinced that his nan's spirit was at large in the house. It was as if she was there looking after him. Often after he'd gone to bed, he felt a force gently tugging at his duvet as if someone was trying to tuck him in for the night.

On one occasion, things had been moved around in his room. Brendan had been tidying up before he had gone to bed. He had hung up two belts and a scarf on an upright mirror in his bedroom. In the middle of the night he was disturbed once more by a strange sense of someone being in the room with him. When he switched on the lights he saw nothing at first. But then as he scanned the room he saw that the belts and the scarf had been moved and were now hanging on the handle of a wardrobe. It was as if someone had been putting things into the order they wanted them.

Brendan went on to develop his psychic skills. And he thanked his grandmother for giving him the strength – and the evidence – to do so.

Sign Language: Through the Eyes of a Child

I believe all children are born open to the spirit world. If children know there are spirits present, they often see them in the form of imaginary friends. I know this from my own experience and that of other mediums like Colin Fry. We have often talked with each other about seeing imaginary friends when we were young, and how we now recognise they were manifestations of spirits.

A friend of mine, Charlotte, has a seven-year-old daughter called Emma. Emma has an imaginary friend who is a seven-year-old boy. When Charlotte asked Emma about him, she pointed at a picture of her elderly granddad who is in the spirit world. Charlotte now knows that when Emma is seeing her imaginary friend, the spirits are present.

I think this phenomenon is down to the fact that the spirit world is trying to protect children. If elderly loved ones were to appear in the form in which they left this earth they might sometimes frighten children. It is far easier for a child to deal with seeing spirits when the spirit takes a form that will be familiar to the child, such as that of another young child. This phenomenon allows those who have crossed over to the spirit world to get close to children.

Epilogue: Nan's Song

I began Christmas Day 2009 with a wish. It wasn't for an expensive present or a new television series, or anything like that. It was simply for a sign from my nan.

It was the first Christmas I'd spent since her passing earlier that year and – once again – she'd been on my mind a great deal. I knew from experience that Christmas is a very sensitive time in this respect. A lot of people come to me during December, hoping to get a message from someone who has passed over. The holiday season seems to make us miss our loved ones more keenly than at any other time of the year. It's understandable. As we gather together as families and friends, we feel the gap they have left in our lives.

In my case, however, it was more than simply missing my nan at Christmas. I needed her help again.

It had been a year of mixed fortunes for me, a real combination of highs and lows. I had seen my first book published, which was something I'd never have imagined possible a few years earlier. But I had also had to go through a difficult patch both in my professional and personal life. There had been a lot of upheaval – and the chances were there would be even more of it ahead in the New Year. The result of all this was that I felt slightly lost. If truth be told I wanted some guidance. And that was why I needed to know that my nan was around. And why I began my Christmas morning by putting out the thought that I needed a sign from her.

The days when I'd had to get up at the crack of dawn on Christmas morning – having gone to bed past midnight on Christmas Eve – had long gone. Now I saw Christmas morning as a nice quiet time, a moment to relax and experience a little peace. So, in order to get a little bit of revenge for all the sleep they'd deprived me of over the years, after sending out my thoughts to my nan, I had woken my boys up reasonably early to hand out their presents to them and then I'd headed back to relax in bed.

We were going over to my dad's for Christmas dinner so I didn't have to worry about cooking a turkey or peeling potatoes. I had made myself a cup of coffee and was looking forward to dipping back into a book that I was particularly enjoying, the story of a girl who received messages from angels.

I always like to have music playing when I read. So I had my iPod plugged into its speakers. But it was just background music and I wasn't really aware of it. I had simply put the iPod on shuffle and let it decide what to play. I was too relaxed to make big decisions like that!

It was only halfway through what must have been the

fifth or sixth song that I realised that it was a repeat of the previous piece of music. I knew the song and the artist. The singer was Robbie Williams but I couldn't put a name to the track. What are the chances of the shuffle setting repeating the same song, I wondered to myself for a moment. But I didn't think anything more of it.

I went back to my book for a minute or two while the song came to an end. But then it started all over again. 'I thought I'd put it on shuffle,' I said to myself this time. 'Why is it playing the same song over and over again?'

It was only when I reached over and looked at the iPod that it struck me what was happening. The names of the artist, the album and the song were displayed on the glass display of the iPod. Yes, as I'd thought, it was from Robbie Williams' album. However, the track was simply called 'Nan's Song'.

My iPod had around 2,500 different pieces of music on it. It could have chosen any one of them. So why did it choose that one? And why then did it choose it not just a second time, but a third time as well? The reason was quite obvious – to me, at least.

As I lay there on Christmas morning I listened carefully to the beautiful lyrics and was suddenly in the company of my beloved and much missed nan, Elsie. She was a great one for Christmas. She also loved her music. She would have appreciated this, I thought. In fact she *was* appreciating it. There was absolutely no doubt in my mind that she was there in the bedroom with me.

The spirit world is with us always. It may not be visible

to us at all times. We may not be able to sense it every minute of every day, but it is there. Sometimes all we have to do is look for it.

All we have to do is to read the signs . . .

Also available from Rider:

LIVING WITH THE GIFT

T J Higgs

'Join me as I connect with the Other Side. Discover how there's more to this life and the next than you ever dreamed possible . . .'

T J Higgs is one of the most celebrated psychic mediums in the UK, whose incredible work has been featured on TV, in hit shows such as 'Psychic Private Eyes' and 'The Three Mediums'.

But she has had to overcome many obstacles to get there. A sensitive child, her unique gift was not encouraged. In fact, she believes that the challenges she has faced have played an essential part in making her the ground-breaking medium she is today.

In this compelling book, T J shares her story along with amazing true tales from the afterlife. Intuitive, witty and wise, she is a very modern medium.